Munro Bagging
Log Book & Journal

The Munros are the mountains in Scotland over 3000 feet high. As you can imagine, the views from each of these peaks is immense – the Scottish Highlands are one of the most beautiful sights in the world. The popularity of 'Munro-bagging' came in the late 1980s and today the numbers are huge. Those who climb all the summits are known as 'compleaters', a feat which only a few have achieved.

This log book is your diary & Journal of Munro Bagging. Record your achievements and memorable moments along the way – a great way to look back on your achievements for years to come.

Walking can be dangerous, you will need a good amount of experience, hill craft and navigation skills before attempting any of the mountains in the list. Attempting the mountains is done entirely at your own risk, and it is your responsibility to properly prepare and navigate using a map and compass.

For your safety before you embark, please use the notes pages at the back of this book to write down your details and any emergency contact information you will need. This includes nearest mountain rescue or emergency service numbers, should you encounter any problems.

A note from the author...

Thank you for buying this book, it really is appreciated as an independent small author. I hope it gives you many years of satisfaction as you bag your Munros!

As an Amazon author, I am constantly looking at user feedback to improve my books - so in this most recent edition you have purchased I have included QR codes for all the mountains wikipedia pages, so you can access further information on your proposed climbs. To access these, simply download a free 'QR scanner' app to your phone and you will be able to access this feature.

I hope you enjoy this latest revision of the book, and if you have any further suggestions of improvements please feel free to email me at: *info@herbertpublishing.com* and I will see what I can do.
Lastly, leaving a review on Amazon for this book really helps independent publishers like me, so would really appreciate a review!
Now off you go and plan your bagging!!!

Lee Herbert – Herbert Publishing

Munro Finder – Height Ascending Order

Full index alphabetical order
at the back of the book

Ben Vane

Height: 915m

Date: ....

Ascent start time: .... Peak time: ....

Descent start time: .... Finish time: ....

Ascent duration: .... Descent duration: ....

Total time: [   ]

Total distance covered:..

Companions:..

....

....

Weather conditions:..

....

Difficulty: (poor) ⭕⭕⭕⭕⭕⭕⭕⭕⭕ (great)

Views: (poor) ⭕⭕⭕⭕⭕⭕⭕⭕⭕ (great)

Enjoyment: (poor) ⭕⭕⭕⭕⭕⭕⭕⭕⭕ (great)

Notes/pics:

Beinn Teallach

Height: 915m

Date: ....

Ascent start time: .... Peak time: ....

Descent start time: .... Finish time: ....

Ascent duration: .... Descent duration: ....

Total time: [   ]

Total distance covered:...

Companions:...

....

....

Weather conditions:...

....

Difficulty: (poor) ○ ○ ○ ○ ○ ○ ○ ○ ○ ○ (great)

Views: (poor) ○ ○ ○ ○ ○ ○ ○ ○ ○ ○ (great)

Enjoyment: (poor) ○ ○ ○ ○ ○ ○ ○ ○ ○ ○ (great)

Notes/pics:

Beinn a'Chleibh

Height: 916m

Date: ....

Ascent start time: .... Peak time: ....

Descent start time: .... Finish time: ....

Ascent duration: .... Descent duration: ....

Total time: [   ]

Total distance covered:..

Companions:..

....

....

Weather conditions:..

....

Difficulty: (poor) ○ ○ ○ ○ ○ ○ ○ ○ ○ (great)

Views: (poor) ○ ○ ○ ○ ○ ○ ○ ○ ○ (great)

Enjoyment: (poor) ○ ○ ○ ○ ○ ○ ○ ○ ○ (great)

Notes/pics:

Geal-charn (Drumochter)

Height: 917m

Date: ....

Ascent start time: .... Peak time: ....

Descent start time: .... Finish time: ....

Ascent duration: .... Descent duration: ....

Total time: [   ]

Total distance covered:..

Companions:...

....

....

Weather conditions:...

....

Difficulty: (poor) ○ ○ ○ ○ ○ ○ ○ ○ ○ ○ (great)

Views: (poor) ○ ○ ○ ○ ○ ○ ○ ○ ○ ○ (great)

Enjoyment: (poor) ○ ○ ○ ○ ○ ○ ○ ○ ○ ○ (great)

Notes/pics:

Carn Aosda

Height: 917m

Date: ....

Ascent start time: .... Peak time: ....

Descent start time: .... Finish time: ....

Ascent duration: .... Descent duration: ....

Total time: [   ]

Total distance covered:..

Companions:..

....

....

Weather conditions:..

....

Difficulty: (poor) ○ ○ ○ ○ ○ ○ ○ ○ ○ ○ (great)

Views: (poor) ○ ○ ○ ○ ○ ○ ○ ○ ○ ○ (great)

Enjoyment: (poor) ○ ○ ○ ○ ○ ○ ○ ○ ○ ○ (great)

Notes/pics:

Sgurr a'Mhadaidh

Height: 918m

Date: ....

Ascent start time: .... Peak time: ....

Descent start time: .... Finish time: ....

Ascent duration: .... Descent duration: ....

Total time: [   ]

Total distance covered: ....

Companions: ....

....

....

Weather conditions: ....

....

Difficulty: (poor) ○ ○ ○ ○ ○ ○ ○ ○ ○ (great)

Views: (poor) ○ ○ ○ ○ ○ ○ ○ ○ ○ (great)

Enjoyment: (poor) ○ ○ ○ ○ ○ ○ ○ ○ ○ (great)

Notes/pics:

Ruadh Stac Mor

Height: 918m

Date: ....

Ascent start time: .... Peak time: ....

Descent start time: .... Finish time: ....

Ascent duration: .... Descent duration: ....

Total time: [   ]

Total distance covered:...

Companions:..

....

....

Weather conditions:..

....

Difficulty: (poor) ○ ○ ○ ○ ○ ○ ○ ○ ○ ○ (great)

Views: (poor) ○ ○ ○ ○ ○ ○ ○ ○ ○ ○ (great)

Enjoyment: (poor) ○ ○ ○ ○ ○ ○ ○ ○ ○ ○ (great)

Notes/pics:

Meall na Teanga

Height: 918m

Date: ....

Ascent start time: .... Peak time: ....

Descent start time: .... Finish time: ....

Ascent duration: .... Descent duration: ....

Total time: [　　　　　　]

Total distance covered:..

Companions:..

....

....

Weather conditions:..

....

Difficulty:　(poor) O O O O O O O O O O (great)

Views:　　(poor) O O O O O O O O O O (great)

Enjoyment: (poor) O O O O O O O O O O (great)

Notes/pics:

Creag nan Damh

Height: 918m

Date: ....

Ascent start time: .... Peak time: ....

Descent start time: .... Finish time: ....

Ascent duration: .... Descent duration: ....

Total time: [   ]

Total distance covered:...

Companions:...

....

....

Weather conditions:...

....

Difficulty: (poor) ○ ○ ○ ○ ○ ○ ○ ○ ○ ○ (great)

Views: (poor) ○ ○ ○ ○ ○ ○ ○ ○ ○ ○ (great)

Enjoyment: (poor) ○ ○ ○ ○ ○ ○ ○ ○ ○ ○ (great)

Notes/pics:

A' Ghlas-bheinn

Height: 918m

Date: ....

Ascent start time: .... Peak time: ....

Descent start time: .... Finish time: ....

Ascent duration: .... Descent duration: ....

Total time: [   ]

Total distance covered:...

Companions:..

....

....

Weather conditions:..

....

Difficulty: (poor) ○ ○ ○ ○ ○ ○ ○ ○ ○ (great)

Views: (poor) ○ ○ ○ ○ ○ ○ ○ ○ ○ (great)

Enjoyment: (poor) ○ ○ ○ ○ ○ ○ ○ ○ ○ (great)

Notes/pics:

Gairich

Height: 919m

Date: ....

Ascent start time: .... Peak time: ....

Descent start time: .... Finish time: ....

Ascent duration: .... Descent duration: ....

Total time: [   ]

Total distance covered:...

Companions:..

....

....

Weather conditions:...

....

Difficulty: (poor) ○ ○ ○ ○ ○ ○ ○ ○ ○ (great)

Views: (poor) ○ ○ ○ ○ ○ ○ ○ ○ ○ (great)

Enjoyment: (poor) ○ ○ ○ ○ ○ ○ ○ ○ ○ (great)

Notes/pics:

Carn Sgulain

Height: 920m

Date: ....

Ascent start time: .... Peak time: ....

Descent start time: .... Finish time: ....

Ascent duration: .... Descent duration: ....

Total time: [   ]

Total distance covered:...

Companions:..

....

....

Weather conditions:...

....

Difficulty: (poor) ○ ○ ○ ○ ○ ○ ○ ○ ○ (great)

Views: (poor) ○ ○ ○ ○ ○ ○ ○ ○ ○ (great)

Enjoyment: (poor) ○ ○ ○ ○ ○ ○ ○ ○ ○ (great)

Notes/pics:

Sgiath Chuil

Height: 921m

Date: ....

Ascent start time: .... Peak time: ....

Descent start time: .... Finish time: ....

Ascent duration: .... Descent duration: ....

Total time:

Total distance covered:...

Companions:..

....

....

Weather conditions:...

....

Difficulty: (poor) ○ ○ ○ ○ ○ ○ ○ ○ ○ (great)

Views: (poor) ○ ○ ○ ○ ○ ○ ○ ○ ○ (great)

Enjoyment: (poor) ○ ○ ○ ○ ○ ○ ○ ○ ○ (great)

Notes/pics:

An Socach (Affric)

Height: 921m

Date: ....

Ascent start time: .... Peak time: ....

Descent start time: .... Finish time: ....

Ascent duration: .... Descent duration: ....

Total time: [   ]

Total distance covered:...

Companions:...

....

....

Weather conditions:...

....

Difficulty: (poor) ○ ○ ○ ○ ○ ○ ○ ○ ○ (great)

Views: (poor) ○ ○ ○ ○ ○ ○ ○ ○ ○ (great)

Enjoyment: (poor) ○ ○ ○ ○ ○ ○ ○ ○ ○ (great)

Notes/pics:

Tom na Gruagaich
(Beinn Alligin)

Height: 922m

Date: ....

Ascent start time: .... Peak time: ....

Descent start time: .... Finish time: ....

Ascent duration: .... Descent duration: ....

Total time: [   ]

Total distance covered:..

Companions:...

....

....

Weather conditions:..

....

Difficulty: (poor) ○ ○ ○ ○ ○ ○ ○ ○ ○ ○ (great)

Views: (poor) ○ ○ ○ ○ ○ ○ ○ ○ ○ ○ (great)

Enjoyment: (poor) ○ ○ ○ ○ ○ ○ ○ ○ ○ ○ (great)

Notes/pics:

Sgurr nan Each

Height: 923m

Date: ....

Ascent start time: .... Peak time: ....

Descent start time: .... Finish time: ....

Ascent duration: .... Descent duration: ....

Total time: [   ]

Total distance covered:...

Companions:...

....

....

Weather conditions:...

....

Difficulty: (poor) ○ ○ ○ ○ ○ ○ ○ ○ ○ (great)

Views: (poor) ○ ○ ○ ○ ○ ○ ○ ○ ○ (great)

Enjoyment: (poor) ○ ○ ○ ○ ○ ○ ○ ○ ○ (great)

Notes/pics:

An Coileachan

Height: 923m

Date: ....

Ascent start time: .... Peak time: ....

Descent start time: .... Finish time: ....

Ascent duration: .... Descent duration: ....

Total time:

Total distance covered: ....

Companions: ....

....

....

Weather conditions: ....

....

Difficulty: (poor) ○ ○ ○ ○ ○ ○ ○ ○ ○ ○ (great)

Views: (poor) ○ ○ ○ ○ ○ ○ ○ ○ ○ ○ (great)

Enjoyment: (poor) ○ ○ ○ ○ ○ ○ ○ ○ ○ ○ (great)

Notes/pics:

Sgurr nan Eag

Height: 924m

Date: ....

Ascent start time: .... Peak time: ....

Descent start time: .... Finish time: ....

Ascent duration: .... Descent duration: ....

Total time: [   ]

Total distance covered: ....

Companions: ....

....

....

Weather conditions: ....

....

Difficulty: (poor) ○ ○ ○ ○ ○ ○ ○ ○ ○ (great)

Views: (poor) ○ ○ ○ ○ ○ ○ ○ ○ ○ (great)

Enjoyment: (poor) ○ ○ ○ ○ ○ ○ ○ ○ ○ (great)

Notes/pics:

Creag Pitridh

Height: 924m

Date: ....

Ascent start time: .... Peak time: ....

Descent start time: .... Finish time: ....

Ascent duration: .... Descent duration: ....

Total time: [ ]

Total distance covered:...

Companions:..

....

....

Weather conditions:...

....

Difficulty: (poor) ○ ○ ○ ○ ○ ○ ○ ○ ○ ○ (great)

Views: (poor) ○ ○ ○ ○ ○ ○ ○ ○ ○ ○ (great)

Enjoyment: (poor) ○ ○ ○ ○ ○ ○ ○ ○ ○ ○ (great)

Notes/pics:

Stob Coire Raineach
(Buachaille Etive Beag)

Height: 925m

Date: ....

Ascent start time: .... Peak time: ....

Descent start time: .... Finish time: ....

Ascent duration: .... Descent duration: ....

Total time: [   ]

Total distance covered:..

Companions:..

....

....

Weather conditions:...

....

Difficulty: (poor) ○ ○ ○ ○ ○ ○ ○ ○ ○ ○ (great)

Views: (poor) ○ ○ ○ ○ ○ ○ ○ ○ ○ ○ (great)

Enjoyment: (poor) ○ ○ ○ ○ ○ ○ ○ ○ ○ ○ (great)

Notes/pics:

Seana Bhraigh

Height: 926m

Date: ....

Ascent start time: .... Peak time: ....

Descent start time: .... Finish time: ....

Ascent duration: .... Descent duration: ....

Total time:

Total distance covered:...

Companions:...

....

....

Weather conditions:...

....

Difficulty: (poor) ○ ○ ○ ○ ○ ○ ○ ○ ○ ○ (great)

Views: (poor) ○ ○ ○ ○ ○ ○ ○ ○ ○ ○ (great)

Enjoyment: (poor) ○ ○ ○ ○ ○ ○ ○ ○ ○ ○ (great)

Notes/pics:

Meall a'Choire Leith

Height: 926m

Date: ....

Ascent start time: .... Peak time: ....

Descent start time: .... Finish time: ....

Ascent duration: .... Descent duration: ....

Total time: [   ]

Total distance covered:...

Companions:...

....

....

Weather conditions:...

....

Difficulty: (poor) ○ ○ ○ ○ ○ ○ ○ ○ ○ ○ (great)

Views: (poor) ○ ○ ○ ○ ○ ○ ○ ○ ○ ○ (great)

Enjoyment: (poor) ○ ○ ○ ○ ○ ○ ○ ○ ○ ○ (great)

Notes/pics:

Geal Charn (Monadhliath)

Height: 926m

Date: ....

Ascent start time: .... Peak time: ....

Descent start time: .... Finish time: ....

Ascent duration: .... Descent duration: ....

Total time: [   ]

Total distance covered: ....

Companions: ....

....

....

Weather conditions: ....

....

Difficulty: (poor) ○ ○ ○ ○ ○ ○ ○ ○ ○ (great)

Views: (poor) ○ ○ ○ ○ ○ ○ ○ ○ ○ (great)

Enjoyment: (poor) ○ ○ ○ ○ ○ ○ ○ ○ ○ (great)

Notes/pics:

Beinn Narnain

Height: 926m

Date: ....

Ascent start time: .... Peak time: ....

Descent start time: .... Finish time: ....

Ascent duration: .... Descent duration: ....

Total time: [   ]

Total distance covered:...

Companions:...

....

....

Weather conditions:..

....

Difficulty: (poor) ○ ○ ○ ○ ○ ○ ○ ○ ○ (great)

Views: (poor) ○ ○ ○ ○ ○ ○ ○ ○ ○ (great)

Enjoyment: (poor) ○ ○ ○ ○ ○ ○ ○ ○ ○ (great)

Notes/pics:

Beinn Liath Mhor

Height: 926m

Date: ....

Ascent start time: .... Peak time: ....

Descent start time: .... Finish time: ....

Ascent duration: .... Descent duration: ....

Total time: [   ]

Total distance covered:...

Companions:...

....

....

Weather conditions:...

....

Difficulty: (poor) ○ ○ ○ ○ ○ ○ ○ ○ ○ ○ (great)

Views: (poor) ○ ○ ○ ○ ○ ○ ○ ○ ○ ○ (great)

Enjoyment: (poor) ○ ○ ○ ○ ○ ○ ○ ○ ○ ○ (great)

Notes/pics:

Eididh nan Clach Geala

Height: 927m

Date: ....
Ascent start time: .... Peak time: ....
Descent start time: .... Finish time: ....

Ascent duration: .... Descent duration: ....
Total time: [   ]
Total distance covered:...
Companions:...
....
....
Weather conditions:..
....

Difficulty: (poor) ○ ○ ○ ○ ○ ○ ○ ○ ○ ○ (great)
Views: (poor) ○ ○ ○ ○ ○ ○ ○ ○ ○ ○ (great)
Enjoyment: (poor) ○ ○ ○ ○ ○ ○ ○ ○ ○ ○ (great)

Notes/pics:

Ben Hope

Height: 927m

Date: ....

Ascent start time: .... Peak time: ....

Descent start time: .... Finish time: ....

Ascent duration: .... Descent duration: ....

Total time:

Total distance covered:...

Companions:...

....

....

Weather conditions:..

....

Difficulty: (poor) ○ ○ ○ ○ ○ ○ ○ ○ ○ ○ (great)

Views: (poor) ○ ○ ○ ○ ○ ○ ○ ○ ○ ○ (great)

Enjoyment: (poor) ○ ○ ○ ○ ○ ○ ○ ○ ○ ○ (great)

Notes/pics:

Moruisg

Height: 928m

Date: ....

Ascent start time: .... Peak time: ....

Descent start time: .... Finish time: ....

Ascent duration: .... Descent duration: ....

Total time: [   ]

Total distance covered:..

Companions:..

....

....

Weather conditions:...

....

Difficulty: (poor) ○ ○ ○ ○ ○ ○ ○ ○ ○ ○ (great)

Views: (poor) ○ ○ ○ ○ ○ ○ ○ ○ ○ ○ (great)

Enjoyment: (poor) ○ ○ ○ ○ ○ ○ ○ ○ ○ ○ (great)

Notes/pics:

Ben Chonzie

Height: 931m

Date: ....

Ascent start time: .... Peak time: ....

Descent start time: .... Finish time: ....

Ascent duration: .... Descent duration: ....

Total time:

Total distance covered:..

Companions:..

....

....

Weather conditions:..

....

Difficulty: (poor) ○ ○ ○ ○ ○ ○ ○ ○ ○ ○ (great)

Views: (poor) ○ ○ ○ ○ ○ ○ ○ ○ ○ ○ (great)

Enjoyment: (poor) ○ ○ ○ ○ ○ ○ ○ ○ ○ ○ (great)

Notes/pics:

Beinn Bhreac

Height: 931m

Date: ....

Ascent start time: .... Peak time: ....

Descent start time: .... Finish time: ....

Ascent duration: .... Descent duration: ....

Total time: [   ]

Total distance covered:...

Companions:...

....

....

Weather conditions:...

....

Difficulty: (poor) ○ ○ ○ ○ ○ ○ ○ ○ ○ (great)

Views: (poor) ○ ○ ○ ○ ○ ○ ○ ○ ○ (great)

Enjoyment: (poor) ○ ○ ○ ○ ○ ○ ○ ○ ○ (great)

Notes/pics:

Meall Buidhe
(Glen Lyon)

Height: 932m

Date: ....

Ascent start time: .... Peak time: ....

Descent start time: .... Finish time: ....

Ascent duration: .... Descent duration: ....

Total time:

Total distance covered:...

Companions:...

....

....

Weather conditions:..

....

Difficulty: (poor) ○ ○ ○ ○ ○ ○ ○ ○ ○ (great)

Views: (poor) ○ ○ ○ ○ ○ ○ ○ ○ ○ (great)

Enjoyment: (poor) ○ ○ ○ ○ ○ ○ ○ ○ ○ (great)

Notes/pics:

The Cairnwell

Height: 933m

Date: ....

Ascent start time: .... Peak time: ....

Descent start time: .... Finish time: ....

Ascent duration: .... Descent duration: ....

Total time: [   ]

Total distance covered:...

Companions:...

....

....

Weather conditions:...

....

Difficulty: (poor) ○ ○ ○ ○ ○ ○ ○ ○ ○ ○ (great)

Views: (poor) ○ ○ ○ ○ ○ ○ ○ ○ ○ ○ (great)

Enjoyment: (poor) ○ ○ ○ ○ ○ ○ ○ ○ ○ ○ (great)

Notes/pics:

Am Basteir

Height: 934m

Date: ....

Ascent start time: .... Peak time: ....

Descent start time: .... Finish time: ....

Ascent duration: .... Descent duration: ....

Total time:

Total distance covered:...

Companions:..

....

....

Weather conditions:...

....

Difficulty: (poor) ○ ○ ○ ○ ○ ○ ○ ○ ○ ○ (great)

Views: (poor) ○ ○ ○ ○ ○ ○ ○ ○ ○ ○ (great)

Enjoyment: (poor) ○ ○ ○ ○ ○ ○ ○ ○ ○ ○ (great)

Notes/pics:

A' Bhuidheanach Bheag

Height: 936m

Date: ....

Ascent start time: .... Peak time: ....

Descent start time: .... Finish time: ....

Ascent duration: .... Descent duration: ....

Total time: [   ]

Total distance covered:...

Companions:...

....

....

Weather conditions:...

....

Difficulty: (poor) ○ ○ ○ ○ ○ ○ ○ ○ ○ ○ (great)

Views: (poor) ○ ○ ○ ○ ○ ○ ○ ○ ○ ○ (great)

Enjoyment: (poor) ○ ○ ○ ○ ○ ○ ○ ○ ○ ○ (great)

Notes/pics:

Sron a'Choire Ghairbh

Height: 937m

Date: ....

Ascent start time: .... Peak time: ....

Descent start time: .... Finish time: ....

Ascent duration: .... Descent duration: ....

Total time:

Total distance covered:...

Companions:...

....

....

Weather conditions:...

....

Difficulty: (poor) ○ ○ ○ ○ ○ ○ ○ ○ ○ ○ (great)

Views: (poor) ○ ○ ○ ○ ○ ○ ○ ○ ○ ○ (great)

Enjoyment: (poor) ○ ○ ○ ○ ○ ○ ○ ○ ○ ○ (great)

Notes/pics:

Beinn Tarsuinn

Height: 937m

Date: ....
Ascent start time: .... Peak time: ....
Descent start time: .... Finish time: ....

Ascent duration: .... Descent duration: ....
Total time: [　　　　　]
Total distance covered:...
Companions:..
....
....
Weather conditions:..
....

Difficulty: (poor) ○ ○ ○ ○ ○ ○ ○ ○ ○ ○ (great)

Views: (poor) ○ ○ ○ ○ ○ ○ ○ ○ ○ ○ (great)

Enjoyment: (poor) ○ ○ ○ ○ ○ ○ ○ ○ ○ ○ (great)

Notes/pics:

Beinn Sgulaird

Height: 937m

Date: ....

Ascent start time: .... Peak time: ....

Descent start time: .... Finish time: ....

Ascent duration: .... Descent duration: ....

Total time:

Total distance covered:...

Companions:..

....

....

Weather conditions:..

....

Difficulty: (poor) ○ ○ ○ ○ ○ ○ ○ ○ ○ ○ (great)

Views: (poor) ○ ○ ○ ○ ○ ○ ○ ○ ○ ○ (great)

Enjoyment: (poor) ○ ○ ○ ○ ○ ○ ○ ○ ○ ○ (great)

Notes/pics:

Beinn na Lap

Height: 937m

Date: ....

Ascent start time: .... Peak time: ....

Descent start time: .... Finish time: ....

Ascent duration: .... Descent duration: ....

Total time: [ ]

Total distance covered:...

Companions:...

....

....

Weather conditions:..

....

Difficulty: (poor) ○ ○ ○ ○ ○ ○ ○ ○ ○ ○ (great)

Views: (poor) ○ ○ ○ ○ ○ ○ ○ ○ ○ ○ (great)

Enjoyment: (poor) ○ ○ ○ ○ ○ ○ ○ ○ ○ ○ (great)

Notes/pics:

Carn Dearg (Corrour)

Height: 941m

Date: ....

Ascent start time: .... Peak time: ....

Descent start time: .... Finish time: ....

Ascent duration: .... Descent duration: ....

Total time:

Total distance covered:...

Companions:..

....

....

Weather conditions:..

....

Difficulty: (poor) ○ ○ ○ ○ ○ ○ ○ ○ ○ ○ (great)

Views: (poor) ○ ○ ○ ○ ○ ○ ○ ○ ○ ○ (great)

Enjoyment: (poor) ○ ○ ○ ○ ○ ○ ○ ○ ○ ○ (great)

Notes/pics:

Beinn a'Chroin

Height: 942m

Date: ....

Ascent start time: .... Peak time: ....

Descent start time: .... Finish time: ....

Ascent duration: .... Descent duration: ....

Total time: [   ]

Total distance covered:..

Companions:...

....

....

Weather conditions:..

....

Difficulty: (poor) ○ ○ ○ ○ ○ ○ ○ ○ ○ ○ (great)

Views: (poor) ○ ○ ○ ○ ○ ○ ○ ○ ○ ○ (great)

Enjoyment: (poor) ○ ○ ○ ○ ○ ○ ○ ○ ○ ○ (great)

Notes/pics:

Binnein Beag

Height: 943m

Date: ....

Ascent start time: .... Peak time: ....

Descent start time: .... Finish time: ....

Ascent duration: .... Descent duration: ....

Total time:

Total distance covered:...

Companions:..

....

....

Weather conditions:...

....

Difficulty: (poor) ○ ○ ○ ○ ○ ○ ○ ○ ○ ○ (great)

Views: (poor) ○ ○ ○ ○ ○ ○ ○ ○ ○ ○ (great)

Enjoyment: (poor) ○ ○ ○ ○ ○ ○ ○ ○ ○ ○ (great)

Notes/pics:

Ben Vorlich
(Loch Lomond)

Height: 943m

Date: ....

Ascent start time: .... Peak time: ....

Descent start time: .... Finish time: ....

Ascent duration: .... Descent duration: ....

Total time: [ ]

Total distance covered:..

Companions:..

....

....

Weather conditions:...

....

Difficulty: (poor) ○ ○ ○ ○ ○ ○ ○ ○ ○ ○ (great)

Views: (poor) ○ ○ ○ ○ ○ ○ ○ ○ ○ ○ (great)

Enjoyment: (poor) ○ ○ ○ ○ ○ ○ ○ ○ ○ ○ (great)

Notes/pics:

Carn Dearg
(Monadhliath)

Height: 945m

Date: ....

Ascent start time: .... Peak time: ....

Descent start time: .... Finish time: ....

Ascent duration: .... Descent duration: ....

Total time: [ ]

Total distance covered:...

Companions:...

....

....

Weather conditions:..

....

Difficulty:　(poor) ○ ○ ○ ○ ○ ○ ○ ○ ○ ○ (great)

Views:　　(poor) ○ ○ ○ ○ ○ ○ ○ ○ ○ ○ (great)

Enjoyment: (poor) ○ ○ ○ ○ ○ ○ ○ ○ ○ ○ (great)

Notes/pics:

Bidein a'Choire Sheasgaich

Height: 945m

Date: ....

Ascent start time: .... Peak time: ....

Descent start time: .... Finish time: ....

Ascent duration: .... Descent duration: ....

Total time: [   ]

Total distance covered:..

Companions:..

....

....

Weather conditions:..

....

Difficulty: (poor) ○ ○ ○ ○ ○ ○ ○ ○ ○ ○ (great)

Views: (poor) ○ ○ ○ ○ ○ ○ ○ ○ ○ ○ (great)

Enjoyment: (poor) ○ ○ ○ ○ ○ ○ ○ ○ ○ ○ (great)

Notes/pics:

Meall Buidhe
(Knoydart)

Height: 946m

Date: ....

Ascent start time: .... Peak time: ....

Descent start time: .... Finish time: ....

Ascent duration: .... Descent duration: ....

Total time: [   ]

Total distance covered:..

Companions:...

....

....

Weather conditions:...

....

Difficulty: (poor) ○ ○ ○ ○ ○ ○ ○ ○ ○ ○ (great)

Views: (poor) ○ ○ ○ ○ ○ ○ ○ ○ ○ ○ (great)

Enjoyment: (poor) ○ ○ ○ ○ ○ ○ ○ ○ ○ ○ (great)

Notes/pics:

Carn Bhac

Height: 946m

Date: ....

Ascent start time: .... Peak time: ....

Descent start time: .... Finish time: ....

Ascent duration: .... Descent duration: ....

Total time: [   ]

Total distance covered:..

Companions:...

....

....

Weather conditions:..

....

Difficulty: (poor) ○ ○ ○ ○ ○ ○ ○ ○ ○ ○ (great)

Views: (poor) ○ ○ ○ ○ ○ ○ ○ ○ ○ ○ (great)

Enjoyment: (poor) ○ ○ ○ ○ ○ ○ ○ ○ ○ ○ (great)

Notes/pics:

Beinn Tulaichean

Height: 946m

Date: ....

Ascent start time: .... Peak time: ....

Descent start time: .... Finish time: ....

Ascent duration: .... Descent duration: ....

Total time: [   ]

Total distance covered:...

Companions:..

....

....

Weather conditions:...

....

Difficulty: (poor) ○ ○ ○ ○ ○ ○ ○ ○ ○ ○ (great)

Views: (poor) ○ ○ ○ ○ ○ ○ ○ ○ ○ ○ (great)

Enjoyment: (poor) ○ ○ ○ ○ ○ ○ ○ ○ ○ ○ (great)

Notes/pics:

Driesh

Height: 947m

Date: ....

Ascent start time: .... Peak time: ....

Descent start time: .... Finish time: ....

Ascent duration: .... Descent duration: ....

Total time: [   ]

Total distance covered:..

Companions:...

....

....

Weather conditions:..

....

Difficulty: (poor) ○ ○ ○ ○ ○ ○ ○ ○ ○ ○ (great)

Views: (poor) ○ ○ ○ ○ ○ ○ ○ ○ ○ ○ (great)

Enjoyment: (poor) ○ ○ ○ ○ ○ ○ ○ ○ ○ ○ (great)

Notes/pics:

Creag a'Mhaim

Height: 947m

Date: ....

Ascent start time: .... Peak time: ....

Descent start time: .... Finish time: ....

Ascent duration: .... Descent duration: ....

Total time: [   ]

Total distance covered:..

Companions:...

....

....

Weather conditions:..

....

Difficulty: (poor) ○ ○ ○ ○ ○ ○ ○ ○ ○ ○ (great)

Views: (poor) ○ ○ ○ ○ ○ ○ ○ ○ ○ ○ (great)

Enjoyment: (poor) ○ ○ ○ ○ ○ ○ ○ ○ ○ ○ (great)

Notes/pics:

Sgurr Mhic Choinnich

Height: 948m

Date: ....

Ascent start time: .... Peak time: ....

Descent start time: .... Finish time: ....

Ascent duration: .... Descent duration: ....

Total time: [   ]

Total distance covered:...

Companions:...

....

....

Weather conditions:..

....

Difficulty:　(poor) ○ ○ ○ ○ ○ ○ ○ ○ ○ ○ (great)

Views:　　　(poor) ○ ○ ○ ○ ○ ○ ○ ○ ○ ○ (great)

Enjoyment: (poor) ○ ○ ○ ○ ○ ○ ○ ○ ○ ○ (great)

Notes/pics:

Beinn Bhuidhe

Height: 948m

Date: ....

Ascent start time: .... Peak time: ....

Descent start time: .... Finish time: ....

Ascent duration: .... Descent duration: ....

Total time: [   ]

Total distance covered:...

Companions:...

....

....

Weather conditions:..

....

Difficulty: (poor) ○ ○ ○ ○ ○ ○ ○ ○ ○ (great)

Views: (poor) ○ ○ ○ ○ ○ ○ ○ ○ ○ (great)

Enjoyment: (poor) ○ ○ ○ ○ ○ ○ ○ ○ ○ (great)

Notes/pics:

Meall Gorm

Height: 949m

Date: ....

Ascent start time: .... Peak time: ....

Descent start time: .... Finish time: ....

Ascent duration: .... Descent duration: ....

Total time: [   ]

Total distance covered:...

Companions:..

....

....

Weather conditions:...

....

Difficulty: (poor) ○ ○ ○ ○ ○ ○ ○ ○ ○ ○ (great)

Views: (poor) ○ ○ ○ ○ ○ ○ ○ ○ ○ ○ (great)

Enjoyment: (poor) ○ ○ ○ ○ ○ ○ ○ ○ ○ ○ (great)

Notes/pics:

Meall Chuaich

Height: 951m

Date: ....

Ascent start time: .... Peak time: ....

Descent start time: .... Finish time: ....

Ascent duration: .... Descent duration: ....

Total time: [   ]

Total distance covered:..

Companions:...

....

....

Weather conditions:..

....

Difficulty: (poor) ○ ○ ○ ○ ○ ○ ○ ○ ○ (great)

Views: (poor) ○ ○ ○ ○ ○ ○ ○ ○ ○ (great)

Enjoyment: (poor) ○ ○ ○ ○ ○ ○ ○ ○ ○ (great)

Notes/pics:

Sgurr nan Coireachan
(Glen Dessary)

Height: 953m

Date: ....

Ascent start time: .... Peak time: ....

Descent start time: .... Finish time: ....

Ascent duration: .... Descent duration: ....

Total time: [ ]

Total distance covered:...

Companions:..

....

....

Weather conditions:..

....

Difficulty: (poor) ○ ○ ○ ○ ○ ○ ○ ○ ○ ○ (great)

Views: (poor) ○ ○ ○ ○ ○ ○ ○ ○ ○ ○ (great)

Enjoyment: (poor) ○ ○ ○ ○ ○ ○ ○ ○ ○ ○ (great)

Notes/pics:

Meall Dearg
(Aonach Eagach)

Height: 953m

Date: ....

Ascent start time: .... Peak time: ....

Descent start time: .... Finish time: ....

Ascent duration: .... Descent duration: ....

Total time: [   ]

Total distance covered:...

Companions:..

....

....

Weather conditions:..

....

Difficulty: (poor) ○ ○ ○ ○ ○ ○ ○ ○ ○ (great)

Views: (poor) ○ ○ ○ ○ ○ ○ ○ ○ ○ (great)

Enjoyment: (poor) ○ ○ ○ ○ ○ ○ ○ ○ ○ (great)

Notes/pics:

Beinn Mhanach

Height: 953m

Date: ....

Ascent start time: .... Peak time: ....

Descent start time: .... Finish time: ....

Ascent duration: .... Descent duration: ....

Total time: [ ]

Total distance covered:...

Companions:..

....

....

Weather conditions:...

....

Difficulty: (poor) ○ ○ ○ ○ ○ ○ ○ ○ ○ ○ (great)

Views: (poor) ○ ○ ○ ○ ○ ○ ○ ○ ○ ○ (great)

Enjoyment: (poor) ○ ○ ○ ○ ○ ○ ○ ○ ○ ○ (great)

Notes/pics:

Beinn Liath
Mhor Fannaich

Height: 954m

Date: ....

Ascent start time: .... Peak time: ....

Descent start time: .... Finish time: ....

Ascent duration: .... Descent duration: ....

Total time: [   ]

Total distance covered:...

Companions:...

....

....

Weather conditions:..

....

Difficulty: (poor) ○ ○ ○ ○ ○ ○ ○ ○ ○ (great)

Views: (poor) ○ ○ ○ ○ ○ ○ ○ ○ ○ (great)

Enjoyment: (poor) ○ ○ ○ ○ ○ ○ ○ ○ ○ (great)

Notes/pics:

Am Faochagach

Height: 954m

Date: ....

Ascent start time: .... Peak time: ....

Descent start time: .... Finish time: ....

Ascent duration: .... Descent duration: ....

Total time: [   ]

Total distance covered:...

Companions:...

....

....

Weather conditions:...

....

Difficulty: (poor) ○ ○ ○ ○ ○ ○ ○ ○ ○ ○ (great)

Views: (poor) ○ ○ ○ ○ ○ ○ ○ ○ ○ ○ (great)

Enjoyment: (poor) ○ ○ ○ ○ ○ ○ ○ ○ ○ ○ (great)

Notes/pics:

Sgor Gaibhre

Height: 955m

Date: ....

Ascent start time: .... Peak time: ....

Descent start time: .... Finish time: ....

Ascent duration: .... Descent duration: ....

Total time: [   ]

Total distance covered: ....

Companions: ....

....

....

Weather conditions: ....

....

Difficulty: (poor) ○ ○ ○ ○ ○ ○ ○ ○ ○ ○ (great)

Views: (poor) ○ ○ ○ ○ ○ ○ ○ ○ ○ ○ (great)

Enjoyment: (poor) ○ ○ ○ ○ ○ ○ ○ ○ ○ ○ (great)

Notes/pics:

Stob na Broige
(Buachaille Etive Mor)

Height: 956m

Date: ....

Ascent start time: .... Peak time: ....

Descent start time: .... Finish time: ....

Ascent duration: .... Descent duration: ....

Total time: [   ]

Total distance covered:...

Companions:...

....

....

Weather conditions:...

....

Difficulty: (poor) ○ ○ ○ ○ ○ ○ ○ ○ ○ ○ (great)

Views: (poor) ○ ○ ○ ○ ○ ○ ○ ○ ○ ○ (great)

Enjoyment: (poor) ○ ○ ○ ○ ○ ○ ○ ○ ○ ○ (great)

Notes/pics:

Stob Dubh
(Buachaille Etive Beag)

Height: 956m

Date: ....

Ascent start time: .... Peak time: ....

Descent start time: .... Finish time: ....

Ascent duration: .... Descent duration: ....

Total time:

Total distance covered:...

Companions:..

....

....

Weather conditions:..

....

Difficulty: (poor) ○ ○ ○ ○ ○ ○ ○ ○ ○ ○ (great)

Views: (poor) ○ ○ ○ ○ ○ ○ ○ ○ ○ ○ (great)

Enjoyment: (poor) ○ ○ ○ ○ ○ ○ ○ ○ ○ ○ (great)

Notes/pics:

Sgurr nan Coireachan (Glenfinnan)

Height: 956m

Date: ....

Ascent start time: .... Peak time: ....

Descent start time: .... Finish time: ....

Ascent duration: .... Descent duration: ....

Total time: [   ]

Total distance covered:...

Companions:..

....

....

Weather conditions:..

....

Difficulty: (poor) ○ ○ ○ ○ ○ ○ ○ ○ ○ ○ (great)

Views: (poor) ○ ○ ○ ○ ○ ○ ○ ○ ○ ○ (great)

Enjoyment: (poor) ○ ○ ○ ○ ○ ○ ○ ○ ○ ○ (great)

Notes/pics:

Saileag

Height: 956m

Date: ....

Ascent start time: .... Peak time: ....

Descent start time: .... Finish time: ....

Ascent duration: .... Descent duration: ....

Total time: [   ]

Total distance covered:..

Companions:..

....

....

Weather conditions:..

....

Difficulty: (poor) ○ ○ ○ ○ ○ ○ ○ ○ ○ ○ (great)

Views: (poor) ○ ○ ○ ○ ○ ○ ○ ○ ○ ○ (great)

Enjoyment: (poor) ○ ○ ○ ○ ○ ○ ○ ○ ○ ○ (great)

Notes/pics:

Tom Buidhe

Height: 957m

Date: ....

Ascent start time: .... Peak time: ....

Descent start time: .... Finish time: ....

Ascent duration: .... Descent duration: ....

Total time: [   ]

Total distance covered:...

Companions:...

....

....

Weather conditions:..

....

Difficulty: (poor) ⭘ ⭘ ⭘ ⭘ ⭘ ⭘ ⭘ ⭘ ⭘ ⭘ (great)

Views: (poor) ⭘ ⭘ ⭘ ⭘ ⭘ ⭘ ⭘ ⭘ ⭘ ⭘ (great)

Enjoyment: (poor) ⭘ ⭘ ⭘ ⭘ ⭘ ⭘ ⭘ ⭘ ⭘ ⭘ (great)

Notes/pics:

Carn Ghluasaid

Height: 957m

Date: ....

Ascent start time: .... Peak time: ....

Descent start time: .... Finish time: ....

Ascent duration: .... Descent duration: ....

Total time: [   ]

Total distance covered:..

Companions:..

....

....

Weather conditions:...

....

Difficulty: (poor) ○ ○ ○ ○ ○ ○ ○ ○ ○ ○ (great)

Views: (poor) ○ ○ ○ ○ ○ ○ ○ ○ ○ ○ (great)

Enjoyment: (poor) ○ ○ ○ ○ ○ ○ ○ ○ ○ ○ (great)

Notes/pics:

Tolmount

Height: 958m

Date: ....

Ascent start time: .... Peak time: ....

Descent start time: .... Finish time: ....

Ascent duration: .... Descent duration: ....

Total time: [   ]

Total distance covered:..

Companions:...

....

....

Weather conditions:...

....

Difficulty: (poor) ○ ○ ○ ○ ○ ○ ○ ○ ○ ○ (great)

Views: (poor) ○ ○ ○ ○ ○ ○ ○ ○ ○ ○ (great)

Enjoyment: (poor) ○ ○ ○ ○ ○ ○ ○ ○ ○ ○ (great)

Notes/pics:

Bruach na Frithe

Height: 958m

Date: ....

Ascent start time: .... Peak time: ....

Descent start time: .... Finish time: ....

Ascent duration: .... Descent duration: ....

Total time: [   ]

Total distance covered:...

Companions:...

....

....

Weather conditions:..

....

Difficulty: (poor) ○ ○ ○ ○ ○ ○ ○ ○ ○ ○ (great)

Views: (poor) ○ ○ ○ ○ ○ ○ ○ ○ ○ ○ (great)

Enjoyment: (poor) ○ ○ ○ ○ ○ ○ ○ ○ ○ ○ (great)

Notes/pics:

Meall Glas

Height: 959m

Date: ....

Ascent start time: .... Peak time: ....

Descent start time: .... Finish time: ....

Ascent duration: .... Descent duration: ....

Total time: [   ]

Total distance covered:..

Companions:..

....

....

Weather conditions:..

....

Difficulty: (poor) ○ ○ ○ ○ ○ ○ ○ ○ ○ ○ (great)

Views: (poor) ○ ○ ○ ○ ○ ○ ○ ○ ○ ○ (great)

Enjoyment: (poor) ○ ○ ○ ○ ○ ○ ○ ○ ○ ○ (great)

Notes/pics:

Beinn Fhionnlaidh

Height: 959m

Date: ....

Ascent start time: .... Peak time: ....

Descent start time: .... Finish time: ....

Ascent duration: .... Descent duration: ....

Total time: [   ]

Total distance covered:...

Companions:...

....

....

Weather conditions:..

....

Difficulty: (poor) ○ ○ ○ ○ ○ ○ ○ ○ ○ (great)

Views: (poor) ○ ○ ○ ○ ○ ○ ○ ○ ○ (great)

Enjoyment: (poor) ○ ○ ○ ○ ○ ○ ○ ○ ○ (great)

Notes/pics:

Stuchd an Lochain

Height: 960m

Date: ....

Ascent start time: .... Peak time: ....

Descent start time: .... Finish time: ....

Ascent duration: .... Descent duration: ....

Total time: [   ]

Total distance covered:..

Companions:...

....

....

Weather conditions:...

....

Difficulty: (poor) ○ ○ ○ ○ ○ ○ ○ ○ ○ ○ (great)

Views: (poor) ○ ○ ○ ○ ○ ○ ○ ○ ○ ○ (great)

Enjoyment: (poor) ○ ○ ○ ○ ○ ○ ○ ○ ○ ○ (great)

Notes/pics:

Beinn nan Aighenan

Height: 960m

Date: ....

Ascent start time: .... Peak time: ....

Descent start time: .... Finish time: ....

Ascent duration: .... Descent duration: ....

Total time: [　　　　　　]

Total distance covered:..

Companions:..

....

....

Weather conditions:..

....

Difficulty: (poor) ○ ○ ○ ○ ○ ○ ○ ○ ○ ○ (great)

Views: (poor) ○ ○ ○ ○ ○ ○ ○ ○ ○ ○ (great)

Enjoyment: (poor) ○ ○ ○ ○ ○ ○ ○ ○ ○ ○ (great)

Notes/pics:

Ben Klibreck

Height: 961m

Date: ....

Ascent start time: .... Peak time: ....

Descent start time: .... Finish time: ....

Ascent duration: .... Descent duration: ....

Total time: [   ]

Total distance covered:...

Companions:...

....

....

Weather conditions:..

....

Difficulty: (poor) ○ ○ ○ ○ ○ ○ ○ ○ ○ (great)

Views: (poor) ○ ○ ○ ○ ○ ○ ○ ○ ○ (great)

Enjoyment: (poor) ○ ○ ○ ○ ○ ○ ○ ○ ○ (great)

Notes/pics:

Sgorr Ruadh

Height: 962m

Date: ....

Ascent start time: .... Peak time: ....

Descent start time: .... Finish time: ....

Ascent duration: .... Descent duration: ....

Total time: [   ]

Total distance covered: ....

Companions: ....

....

....

Weather conditions: ....

....

Difficulty: (poor) ○ ○ ○ ○ ○ ○ ○ ○ ○ (great)

Views: (poor) ○ ○ ○ ○ ○ ○ ○ ○ ○ (great)

Enjoyment: (poor) ○ ○ ○ ○ ○ ○ ○ ○ ○ (great)

Notes/pics:

Sgurr Thuilm

Height: 963m

Date: ....

Ascent start time: .... Peak time: ....

Descent start time: .... Finish time: ....

Ascent duration: .... Descent duration: ....

Total time: ⬚

Total distance covered: ....

Companions: ....

....

....

Weather conditions: ....

....

Difficulty: (poor) ○ ○ ○ ○ ○ ○ ○ ○ ○ ○ (great)

Views: (poor) ○ ○ ○ ○ ○ ○ ○ ○ ○ ○ (great)

Enjoyment: (poor) ○ ○ ○ ○ ○ ○ ○ ○ ○ ○ (great)

Notes/pics:

Carn a'Chlamain

Height: 963m

Date: ....

Ascent start time: .... Peak time: ....

Descent start time: .... Finish time: ....

Ascent duration: .... Descent duration: ....

Total time: [   ]

Total distance covered:...

Companions:...

....

....

Weather conditions:..

....

Difficulty: (poor) ○ ○ ○ ○ ○ ○ ○ ○ ○ ○ (great)

Views: (poor) ○ ○ ○ ○ ○ ○ ○ ○ ○ ○ (great)

Enjoyment: (poor) ○ ○ ○ ○ ○ ○ ○ ○ ○ ○ (great)

Notes/pics:

Sgurr nan Gillean

Height: 964m

Date: ....

Ascent start time: .... Peak time: ....

Descent start time: .... Finish time: ....

Ascent duration: .... Descent duration: ....

Total time: [   ]

Total distance covered: ....

Companions: ....

....

....

Weather conditions: ....

....

Difficulty: (poor) ○ ○ ○ ○ ○ ○ ○ ○ ○ ○ (great)

Views: (poor) ○ ○ ○ ○ ○ ○ ○ ○ ○ ○ (great)

Enjoyment: (poor) ○ ○ ○ ○ ○ ○ ○ ○ ○ ○ (great)

Notes/pics:

Sgurr na Banachdich

Height: 965m

Date: ....

Ascent start time: .... Peak time: ....

Descent start time: .... Finish time: ....

Ascent duration: .... Descent duration: ....

Total time: [   ]

Total distance covered:..

Companions:..

....

....

Weather conditions:...

....

Difficulty: (poor) ○ ○ ○ ○ ○ ○ ○ ○ ○ ○ (great)

Views: (poor) ○ ○ ○ ○ ○ ○ ○ ○ ○ ○ (great)

Enjoyment: (poor) ○ ○ ○ ○ ○ ○ ○ ○ ○ ○ (great)

Notes/pics:

Ben More (Mull)

Height: 966m

Date: ....

Ascent start time: .... Peak time: ....

Descent start time: .... Finish time: ....

Ascent duration: .... Descent duration: ....

Total time: [   ]

Total distance covered:...

Companions:...

....

....

Weather conditions:..

....

Difficulty: (poor) ○ ○ ○ ○ ○ ○ ○ ○ ○ ○ (great)

Views: (poor) ○ ○ ○ ○ ○ ○ ○ ○ ○ ○ (great)

Enjoyment: (poor) ○ ○ ○ ○ ○ ○ ○ ○ ○ ○ (great)

Notes/pics:

Sgorr nam Fiannaidh
(Aonach Eagach)

Height: 967m

Date: ....

Ascent start time: .... Peak time: ....

Descent start time: .... Finish time: ....

Ascent duration: .... Descent duration: ....

Total time: [   ]

Total distance covered: ....

Companions: ....

....

....

Weather conditions: ....

....

Difficulty: (poor) ○ ○ ○ ○ ○ ○ ○ ○ ○ (great)

Views: (poor) ○ ○ ○ ○ ○ ○ ○ ○ ○ (great)

Enjoyment: (poor) ○ ○ ○ ○ ○ ○ ○ ○ ○ (great)

Notes/pics:

A' Mhaighdean

Height: 967m

Date: ....

Ascent start time: .... Peak time: ....

Descent start time: .... Finish time: ....

Ascent duration: .... Descent duration: ....

Total time: [   ]

Total distance covered:...

Companions:...

....

....

Weather conditions:..

....

Difficulty: (poor) ○ ○ ○ ○ ○ ○ ○ ○ ○ ○ (great)

Views: (poor) ○ ○ ○ ○ ○ ○ ○ ○ ○ ○ (great)

Enjoyment: (poor) ○ ○ ○ ○ ○ ○ ○ ○ ○ ○ (great)

Notes/pics:

Meall Garbh
(Carn Mairg)

Height: 968m

Date: ....

Ascent start time: .... Peak time: ....

Descent start time: .... Finish time: ....

Ascent duration: .... Descent duration: ....

Total time: [   ]

Total distance covered:...

Companions:..

....

....

Weather conditions:..

....

Difficulty: (poor) ○ ○ ○ ○ ○ ○ ○ ○ ○ (great)

Views: (poor) ○ ○ ○ ○ ○ ○ ○ ○ ○ (great)

Enjoyment: (poor) ○ ○ ○ ○ ○ ○ ○ ○ ○ (great)

Notes/pics:

Sgurr a'Ghreadaidh

Height: 973m

Date: ....

Ascent start time: .... Peak time: ....

Descent start time: .... Finish time: ....

Ascent duration: .... Descent duration: ....

Total time: [ ]

Total distance covered:..

Companions:..

....

....

Weather conditions:...

....

Difficulty: (poor) ○ ○ ○ ○ ○ ○ ○ ○ ○ (great)

Views: (poor) ○ ○ ○ ○ ○ ○ ○ ○ ○ (great)

Enjoyment: (poor) ○ ○ ○ ○ ○ ○ ○ ○ ○ (great)

Notes/pics:

Ben Lomond

Height: 974m

Date: ....

Ascent start time: .... Peak time: ....

Descent start time: .... Finish time: ....

Ascent duration: .... Descent duration: ....

Total time: [   ]

Total distance covered:..

Companions:...

....

....

Weather conditions:..

....

Difficulty: (poor) ○ ○ ○ ○ ○ ○ ○ ○ ○ ○ (great)

Views: (poor) ○ ○ ○ ○ ○ ○ ○ ○ ○ ○ (great)

Enjoyment: (poor) ○ ○ ○ ○ ○ ○ ○ ○ ○ ○ (great)

Notes/pics:

Beinn Sgritheall

Height: 974m

Date: ....

Ascent start time: .... Peak time: ....

Descent start time: .... Finish time: ....

Ascent duration: .... Descent duration: ....

Total time: [   ]

Total distance covered:...

Companions:...

....

....

Weather conditions:...

....

Difficulty: (poor) ○ ○ ○ ○ ○ ○ ○ ○ ○ ○ (great)

Views: (poor) ○ ○ ○ ○ ○ ○ ○ ○ ○ ○ (great)

Enjoyment: (poor) ○ ○ ○ ○ ○ ○ ○ ○ ○ ○ (great)

Notes/pics:

Stuc a'Chroin

Height: 975m

Date: ....

Ascent start time: .... Peak time: ....

Descent start time: .... Finish time: ....

Ascent duration: .... Descent duration: ....

Total time: [   ]

Total distance covered:...

Companions:...

....

....

Weather conditions:..

....

Difficulty: (poor) ○○○○○○○○○ (great)

Views: (poor) ○○○○○○○○○ (great)

Enjoyment: (poor) ○○○○○○○○○ (great)

Notes/pics:

Carn Liath
(Beinn a'Ghlo)

Height: 975m

Date: ....

Ascent start time: .... Peak time: ....

Descent start time: .... Finish time: ....

Ascent duration: .... Descent duration: ....

Total time: [   ]

Total distance covered:..

Companions:..

....

....

Weather conditions:..

....

Difficulty: (poor) O O O O O O O O O (great)

Views: (poor) O O O O O O O O O (great)

Enjoyment: (poor) O O O O O O O O O (great)

Notes/pics:

Carn a'Gheoidh

Height: 975m

Date: ....

Ascent start time: .... Peak time: ....

Descent start time: .... Finish time: ....

Ascent duration: .... Descent duration: ....

Total time: [   ]

Total distance covered:...

Companions:..

....

....

Weather conditions:..

....

Difficulty: (poor) ○ ○ ○ ○ ○ ○ ○ ○ ○ ○ (great)

Views: (poor) ○ ○ ○ ○ ○ ○ ○ ○ ○ ○ (great)

Enjoyment: (poor) ○ ○ ○ ○ ○ ○ ○ ○ ○ ○ (great)

Notes/pics:

A' Mharconaich

Height: 975m

Date: ....

Ascent start time: .... Peak time: ....

Descent start time: .... Finish time: ....

Ascent duration: .... Descent duration: ....

Total time: [   ]

Total distance covered:...

Companions:...

....

....

Weather conditions:..

....

Difficulty: (poor) ○ ○ ○ ○ ○ ○ ○ ○ ○ ○ (great)

Views: (poor) ○ ○ ○ ○ ○ ○ ○ ○ ○ ○ (great)

Enjoyment: (poor) ○ ○ ○ ○ ○ ○ ○ ○ ○ ○ (great)

Notes/pics:

Stob Ban
(Grey Corries)

Height: 977m

Date: ....

Ascent start time: .... Peak time: ....

Descent start time: .... Finish time: ....

Ascent duration: .... Descent duration: ....

Total time: [   ]

Total distance covered:...

Companions:..

....

....

Weather conditions:...

....

Difficulty: (poor) ○ ○ ○ ○ ○ ○ ○ ○ ○ ○ (great)

Views: (poor) ○ ○ ○ ○ ○ ○ ○ ○ ○ ○ (great)

Enjoyment: (poor) ○ ○ ○ ○ ○ ○ ○ ○ ○ ○ (great)

Notes/pics:

Meall nan Ceapraichean

Height: 977m

Date: ....

Ascent start time: .... Peak time: ....

Descent start time: .... Finish time: ....

Ascent duration: .... Descent duration: ....

Total time: [   ]

Total distance covered:...

Companions:..

....

....

Weather conditions:..

....

Difficulty: (poor) O O O O O O O O O (great)

Views: (poor) O O O O O O O O O (great)

Enjoyment: (poor) O O O O O O O O O (great)

Notes/pics:

Cona' Mheall

Height: 978m

Date: ....

Ascent start time: .... Peak time: ....

Descent start time: .... Finish time: ....

Ascent duration: .... Descent duration: ....

Total time: [   ]

Total distance covered:...

Companions:..

....

....

Weather conditions:..

....

Difficulty: (poor) ○ ○ ○ ○ ○ ○ ○ ○ ○ ○ (great)

Views: (poor) ○ ○ ○ ○ ○ ○ ○ ○ ○ ○ (great)

Enjoyment: (poor) ○ ○ ○ ○ ○ ○ ○ ○ ○ ○ (great)

Notes/pics:

Beinn Dubhchraig

Height: 978m

Date: ....
Ascent start time: .... Peak time: ....
Descent start time: .... Finish time: ....

Ascent duration: .... Descent duration: ....

Total time: [   ]

Total distance covered:..

Companions:...

....

....

Weather conditions:..

....

Difficulty: (poor) ○ ○ ○ ○ ○ ○ ○ ○ ○ ○ (great)

Views: (poor) ○ ○ ○ ○ ○ ○ ○ ○ ○ ○ (great)

Enjoyment: (poor) ○ ○ ○ ○ ○ ○ ○ ○ ○ ○ (great)

Notes/pics:

Stob Coire Sgriodain

Height: 979m

Date: ....

Ascent start time: .... Peak time: ....

Descent start time: .... Finish time: ....

Ascent duration: .... Descent duration: ....

Total time: [   ]

Total distance covered:..

Companions:...

....

....

Weather conditions:..

....

Difficulty: (poor) ○ ○ ○ ○ ○ ○ ○ ○ ○ (great)

Views: (poor) ○ ○ ○ ○ ○ ○ ○ ○ ○ (great)

Enjoyment: (poor) ○ ○ ○ ○ ○ ○ ○ ○ ○ (great)

Notes/pics:

Ciste Dhubh

Height: 979m

Date: ....

Ascent start time: .... Peak time: ....

Descent start time: .... Finish time: ....

Ascent duration: .... Descent duration: ....

Total time: [   ]

Total distance covered:...

Companions:...

....

....

Weather conditions:...

....

Difficulty: (poor) ○ ○ ○ ○ ○ ○ ○ ○ ○ ○ (great)

Views: (poor) ○ ○ ○ ○ ○ ○ ○ ○ ○ ○ (great)

Enjoyment: (poor) ○ ○ ○ ○ ○ ○ ○ ○ ○ ○ (great)

Notes/pics:

Beinn a'Chochuill

Height: 980m

Date: ....

Ascent start time: .... Peak time: ....

Descent start time: .... Finish time: ....

Ascent duration: .... Descent duration: ....

Total time:

Total distance covered:...

Companions:...

....

....

Weather conditions:...

....

Difficulty: (poor) ○ ○ ○ ○ ○ ○ ○ ○ ○ ○ (great)

Views: (poor) ○ ○ ○ ○ ○ ○ ○ ○ ○ ○ (great)

Enjoyment: (poor) ○ ○ ○ ○ ○ ○ ○ ○ ○ ○ (great)

Notes/pics:

Stob Coire a'Chairn

Height: 981m

Date: ....

Ascent start time: .... Peak time: ....

Descent start time: .... Finish time: ....

Ascent duration: .... Descent duration: ....

Total time: [   ]

Total distance covered:..

Companions:...

....

....

Weather conditions:..

....

Difficulty: (poor) ○ ○ ○ ○ ○ ○ ○ ○ ○ (great)

Views: (poor) ○ ○ ○ ○ ○ ○ ○ ○ ○ (great)

Enjoyment: (poor) ○ ○ ○ ○ ○ ○ ○ ○ ○ (great)

Notes/pics:

Slioch

Height: 981m

Date: ....
Ascent start time: .... Peak time: ....
Descent start time: .... Finish time: ....

Ascent duration: .... Descent duration: ....

Total time: [   ]

Total distance covered:...

Companions:...

....

....

Weather conditions:...

....

Difficulty: (poor) ○ ○ ○ ○ ○ ○ ○ ○ ○ ○ (great)

Views: (poor) ○ ○ ○ ○ ○ ○ ○ ○ ○ ○ (great)

Enjoyment: (poor) ○ ○ ○ ○ ○ ○ ○ ○ ○ ○ (great)

Notes/pics:

Maol chinn-dearg

Height: 981m

Date: ....
Ascent start time: .... Peak time: ....
Descent start time: .... Finish time: ....

Ascent duration: .... Descent duration: ....

Total time: [   ]

Total distance covered:...

Companions:..

....

....

Weather conditions:...

....

Difficulty: (poor) O O O O O O O O O (great)

Views: (poor) O O O O O O O O O (great)

Enjoyment: (poor) O O O O O O O O O (great)

Notes/pics:

Creag Mhor
(Meall na Aighean)

Height: 981m

Date: ....

Ascent start time: .... Peak time: ....

Descent start time: .... Finish time: ....

Ascent duration: .... Descent duration: ....

Total time: [   ]

Total distance covered:..

Companions:...

....

....

Weather conditions:..

....

Difficulty: (poor) ○ ○ ○ ○ ○ ○ ○ ○ ○ ○ (great)

Views: (poor) ○ ○ ○ ○ ○ ○ ○ ○ ○ ○ (great)

Enjoyment: (poor) ○ ○ ○ ○ ○ ○ ○ ○ ○ ○ (great)

Notes/pics:

Mullach nan Dheiragain

Height: 982m

Date: ....

Ascent start time: .... Peak time: ....

Descent start time: .... Finish time: ....

Ascent duration: .... Descent duration: ....

Total time: [   ]

Total distance covered:..

Companions:..

....

....

Weather conditions:..

....

Difficulty: (poor) ⊙ ⊙ ⊙ ⊙ ⊙ ⊙ ⊙ ⊙ ⊙ (great)

Views: (poor) ⊙ ⊙ ⊙ ⊙ ⊙ ⊙ ⊙ ⊙ ⊙ (great)

Enjoyment: (poor) ⊙ ⊙ ⊙ ⊙ ⊙ ⊙ ⊙ ⊙ ⊙ (great)

Notes/pics:

An Gearanach

Height: 982m

Date: ....

Ascent start time: .... Peak time: ....

Descent start time: .... Finish time: ....

Ascent duration: .... Descent duration: ....

Total time: [   ]

Total distance covered:..

Companions:..

....

....

Weather conditions:...

....

Difficulty: (poor) ○ ○ ○ ○ ○ ○ ○ ○ ○ ○ (great)

Views: (poor) ○ ○ ○ ○ ○ ○ ○ ○ ○ ○ (great)

Enjoyment: (poor) ○ ○ ○ ○ ○ ○ ○ ○ ○ ○ (great)

Notes/pics:

Ben Vorlich
(Loch Earn)

Height: 985m

Date: ....

Ascent start time: .... Peak time: ....

Descent start time: .... Finish time: ....

Ascent duration: .... Descent duration: ....

Total time: [   ]

Total distance covered:..

Companions:..

....

....

Weather conditions:..

....

Difficulty: (poor) ○ ○ ○ ○ ○ ○ ○ ○ ○ (great)

Views: (poor) ○ ○ ○ ○ ○ ○ ○ ○ ○ (great)

Enjoyment: (poor) ○ ○ ○ ○ ○ ○ ○ ○ ○ (great)

Notes/pics:

Sgurr Mor
(Beinn Alligin)

Height: 986m

Date: ....

Ascent start time: .... Peak time: ....

Descent start time: .... Finish time: ....

Ascent duration: .... Descent duration: ....

Total time:

Total distance covered:...

Companions:..

....

....

Weather conditions:...

....

Difficulty: (poor) ○ ○ ○ ○ ○ ○ ○ ○ ○ ○ (great)

Views: (poor) ○ ○ ○ ○ ○ ○ ○ ○ ○ ○ (great)

Enjoyment: (poor) ○ ○ ○ ○ ○ ○ ○ ○ ○ ○ (great)

Notes/pics:

Lurg Mhor

Height: 986m

Date: ....

Ascent start time: .... Peak time: ....

Descent start time: .... Finish time: ....

Ascent duration: .... Descent duration: ....

Total time:

Total distance covered:...

Companions:...

....

....

Weather conditions:...

....

Difficulty: (poor) ○ ○ ○ ○ ○ ○ ○ ○ ○ ○ (great)

Views: (poor) ○ ○ ○ ○ ○ ○ ○ ○ ○ ○ (great)

Enjoyment: (poor) ○ ○ ○ ○ ○ ○ ○ ○ ○ ○ (great)

Notes/pics:

Inaccessible Pinnacle

Height: 986m

Date: ....

Ascent start time: .... Peak time: ....

Descent start time: .... Finish time: ....

Ascent duration: .... Descent duration: ....

Total time: [   ]

Total distance covered:...

Companions:..

....

....

Weather conditions:...

....

Difficulty: (poor) ○ ○ ○ ○ ○ ○ ○ ○ ○ (great)

Views: (poor) ○ ○ ○ ○ ○ ○ ○ ○ ○ (great)

Enjoyment: (poor) ○ ○ ○ ○ ○ ○ ○ ○ ○ (great)

Notes/pics:

Gulvain

Height: 987m

Date: ....
Ascent start time: .... Peak time: ....
Descent start time: .... Finish time: ....

Ascent duration: .... Descent duration: ....

Total time: [   ]

Total distance covered:...

Companions:...

....

....

Weather conditions:...

....

- Difficulty: (poor) ○ ○ ○ ○ ○ ○ ○ ○ ○ ○ (great)
- Views: (poor) ○ ○ ○ ○ ○ ○ ○ ○ ○ ○ (great)
- Enjoyment: (poor) ○ ○ ○ ○ ○ ○ ○ ○ ○ ○ (great)

Notes/pics:

Druim Shionnach

Height: 987m

Date: ....

Ascent start time: .... Peak time: ....

Descent start time: .... Finish time: ....

Ascent duration: .... Descent duration: ....

Total time: [   ]

Total distance covered:..

Companions:..

....

....

Weather conditions:...

....

Difficulty: (poor) ○ ○ ○ ○ ○ ○ ○ ○ ○ ○ (great)

Views: (poor) ○ ○ ○ ○ ○ ○ ○ ○ ○ ○ (great)

Enjoyment: (poor) ○ ○ ○ ○ ○ ○ ○ ○ ○ ○ (great)

Notes/pics:

Creag Leacach

Height: 987m

Date: ....

Ascent start time: .... Peak time: ....

Descent start time: .... Finish time: ....

Ascent duration: .... Descent duration: ....

Total time: [   ]

Total distance covered:...

Companions:...

....

....

Weather conditions:...

....

Difficulty: (poor) ○ ○ ○ ○ ○ ○ ○ ○ ○ (great)

Views: (poor) ○ ○ ○ ○ ○ ○ ○ ○ ○ (great)

Enjoyment: (poor) ○ ○ ○ ○ ○ ○ ○ ○ ○ (great)

Notes/pics:

Conival

Height: 987m

Date: ....

Ascent start time: .... Peak time: ....

Descent start time: .... Finish time: ....

Ascent duration: .... Descent duration: ....

Total time: [   ]

Total distance covered:...

Companions:...

....

....

Weather conditions:...

....

Difficulty: (poor) ○ ○ ○ ○ ○ ○ ○ ○ ○ (great)

Views: (poor) ○ ○ ○ ○ ○ ○ ○ ○ ○ (great)

Enjoyment: (poor) ○ ○ ○ ○ ○ ○ ○ ○ ○ (great)

Notes/pics:

Sgurr Ban

Height: 989m

Date: ....
Ascent start time: .... Peak time: ....
Descent start time: .... Finish time: ....

Ascent duration: .... Descent duration: ....

Total time: [   ]

Total distance covered:..

Companions:...

....

....

Weather conditions:...

....

Difficulty:　(poor) ○ ○ ○ ○ ○ ○ ○ ○ ○ ○ (great)

Views:　　　(poor) ○ ○ ○ ○ ○ ○ ○ ○ ○ ○ (great)

Enjoyment: (poor) ○ ○ ○ ○ ○ ○ ○ ○ ○ ○ (great)

Notes/pics:

Beinn Eunaich

Height: 989m

Date: ....

Ascent start time: .... Peak time: ....

Descent start time: .... Finish time: ....

Ascent duration: .... Descent duration: ....

Total time:

Total distance covered:..

Companions:...

....

....

Weather conditions:...

....

Difficulty: (poor) ○ ○ ○ ○ ○ ○ ○ ○ ○ (great)

Views: (poor) ○ ○ ○ ○ ○ ○ ○ ○ ○ (great)

Enjoyment: (poor) ○ ○ ○ ○ ○ ○ ○ ○ ○ (great)

Notes/pics:

Sgairneach Mhor

Height: 991m

Date: ....

Ascent start time: .... Peak time: ....

Descent start time: .... Finish time: ....

Ascent duration: .... Descent duration: ....

Total time: [ ]

Total distance covered:...

Companions:..

....

....

Weather conditions:...

....

Difficulty: (poor) ○ ○ ○ ○ ○ ○ ○ ○ ○ ○ (great)

Views: (poor) ○ ○ ○ ○ ○ ○ ○ ○ ○ ○ (great)

Enjoyment: (poor) ○ ○ ○ ○ ○ ○ ○ ○ ○ ○ (great)

Notes/pics:

Sgurr Alasdair

Height: 992m

Date: ....

Ascent start time: .... Peak time: ....

Descent start time: .... Finish time: ....

Ascent duration: .... Descent duration: ....

Total time:

Total distance covered:..

Companions:..

....

....

Weather conditions:...

....

Difficulty: (poor) ○ ○ ○ ○ ○ ○ ○ ○ ○ ○ (great)

Views: (poor) ○ ○ ○ ○ ○ ○ ○ ○ ○ ○ (great)

Enjoyment: (poor) ○ ○ ○ ○ ○ ○ ○ ○ ○ ○ (great)

Notes/pics:

Carn nan Gobhar
(Strathfarrar)

Height: 992m

Date: ....

Ascent start time: .... Peak time: ....

Descent start time: .... Finish time: ....

Ascent duration: .... Descent duration: ....

Total time: [   ]

Total distance covered:..

Companions:...

....

....

Weather conditions:..

....

Difficulty: (poor) ○ ○ ○ ○ ○ ○ ○ ○ ○ ○ (great)

Views: (poor) ○ ○ ○ ○ ○ ○ ○ ○ ○ ○ (great)

Enjoyment: (poor) ○ ○ ○ ○ ○ ○ ○ ○ ○ ○ (great)

Notes/pics:

Carn nan Gobhar
(Loch Mullardoch)

Height: 992m

Date: ....

Ascent start time: .... Peak time: ....

Descent start time: .... Finish time: ....

Ascent duration: .... Descent duration: ....

Total time:

Total distance covered: ....

Companions: ....

....

....

Weather conditions: ....

....

Difficulty: (poor) ○ ○ ○ ○ ○ ○ ○ ○ ○ ○ (great)

Views: (poor) ○ ○ ○ ○ ○ ○ ○ ○ ○ ○ (great)

Enjoyment: (poor) ○ ○ ○ ○ ○ ○ ○ ○ ○ ○ (great)

Notes/pics:

Spidean Coire nan Clach (Beinn Eighe)

Height: 993m

Date: ....

Ascent start time: .... Peak time: ....

Descent start time: .... Finish time: ....

Ascent duration: .... Descent duration: ....

Total time: [   ]

Total distance covered:..

Companions:..

....

....

Weather conditions:...

....

Difficulty: (poor) ○ ○ ○ ○ ○ ○ ○ ○ ○ ○ (great)

Views: (poor) ○ ○ ○ ○ ○ ○ ○ ○ ○ ○ (great)

Enjoyment: (poor) ○ ○ ○ ○ ○ ○ ○ ○ ○ ○ (great)

Notes/pics:

Sgurr na Ruaidhe

Height: 993m

Date: ....

Ascent start time: .... Peak time: ....

Descent start time: .... Finish time: ....

Ascent duration: .... Descent duration: ....

Total time: [   ]

Total distance covered:..

Companions:..

....

....

Weather conditions:..

....

Difficulty: (poor) ○ ○ ○ ○ ○ ○ ○ ○ ○ (great)

Views: (poor) ○ ○ ○ ○ ○ ○ ○ ○ ○ (great)

Enjoyment: (poor) ○ ○ ○ ○ ○ ○ ○ ○ ○ (great)

Notes/pics:

Sgor na h-Ulaidh

Height: 994m

Date: ....
Ascent start time: .... Peak time: ....
Descent start time: .... Finish time: ....

Ascent duration: .... Descent duration: ....

Total time: [   ]

Total distance covered:...

Companions:..

....

....

Weather conditions:...

....

Difficulty: (poor) ○ ○ ○ ○ ○ ○ ○ ○ ○ (great)

Views: (poor) ○ ○ ○ ○ ○ ○ ○ ○ ○ (great)

Enjoyment: (poor) ○ ○ ○ ○ ○ ○ ○ ○ ○ (great)

Notes/pics:

Carn an Fhidhleir
(Carn Ealar)

Height: 994m

Date: ....

Ascent start time: .... Peak time: ....

Descent start time: .... Finish time: ....

Ascent duration: .... Descent duration: ....

Total time: [   ]

Total distance covered:..

Companions:..

....

....

Weather conditions:...

....

Difficulty: (poor) ○ ○ ○ ○ ○ ○ ○ ○ ○ ○ (great)

Views: (poor) ○ ○ ○ ○ ○ ○ ○ ○ ○ ○ (great)

Enjoyment: (poor) ○ ○ ○ ○ ○ ○ ○ ○ ○ ○ (great)

Notes/pics:

An Caisteal

Height: 995m

Date: ....

Ascent start time: .... Peak time: ....

Descent start time: .... Finish time: ....

Ascent duration: .... Descent duration: ....

Total time: [   ]

Total distance covered:..

Companions:...

....

....

Weather conditions:...

....

Difficulty: (poor) ○ ○ ○ ○ ○ ○ ○ ○ ○ ○ (great)

Views: (poor) ○ ○ ○ ○ ○ ○ ○ ○ ○ ○ (great)

Enjoyment: (poor) ○ ○ ○ ○ ○ ○ ○ ○ ○ ○ (great)

Notes/pics:

Spidean Mialach

Height: 996m

Date: ....

Ascent start time: .... Peak time: ....

Descent start time: .... Finish time: ....

Ascent duration: .... Descent duration: ....

Total time: [   ]

Total distance covered: ....

Companions: ....

....

....

Weather conditions: ....

....

Difficulty: (poor) ○ ○ ○ ○ ○ ○ ○ ○ ○ ○ (great)

Views: (poor) ○ ○ ○ ○ ○ ○ ○ ○ ○ ○ (great)

Enjoyment: (poor) ○ ○ ○ ○ ○ ○ ○ ○ ○ ○ (great)

Notes/pics:

Glas Bheinn Mhor

Height: 997m

Date: ....

Ascent start time: .... Peak time: ....

Descent start time: .... Finish time: ....

Ascent duration: .... Descent duration: ....

Total time: [   ]

Total distance covered:..

Companions:..

....

....

Weather conditions:..

....

Difficulty: (poor) ○ ○ ○ ○ ○ ○ ○ ○ ○ ○ (great)

Views: (poor) ○ ○ ○ ○ ○ ○ ○ ○ ○ ○ (great)

Enjoyment: (poor) ○ ○ ○ ○ ○ ○ ○ ○ ○ ○ (great)

Notes/pics:

A' Chailleach

Height: 997m

Date: ....

Ascent start time: .... Peak time: ....

Descent start time: .... Finish time: ....

Ascent duration: .... Descent duration: ....

Total time: [   ]

Total distance covered:...

Companions:...

....

....

Weather conditions:...

....

Difficulty: (poor) ○ ○ ○ ○ ○ ○ ○ ○ ○ ○ (great)

Views: (poor) ○ ○ ○ ○ ○ ○ ○ ○ ○ ○ (great)

Enjoyment: (poor) ○ ○ ○ ○ ○ ○ ○ ○ ○ ○ (great)

Notes/pics:

Stob Daimh

Height: 998m

Date: ....

Ascent start time: .... Peak time: ....

Descent start time: .... Finish time: ....

Ascent duration: .... Descent duration: ....

Total time: [   ]

Total distance covered:...

Companions:..

....

....

Weather conditions:..

....

Difficulty: (poor) O O O O O O O O O O (great)

Views: (poor) O O O O O O O O O O (great)

Enjoyment: (poor) O O O O O O O O O O (great)

Notes/pics:

Broad Cairn

Height: 998m

Date: ....

Ascent start time: .... Peak time: ....

Descent start time: .... Finish time: ....

Ascent duration: .... Descent duration: ....

Total time:

Total distance covered:...

Companions:..

....

....

Weather conditions:..

....

Difficulty: (poor) ○ ○ ○ ○ ○ ○ ○ ○ ○ ○ (great)

Views: (poor) ○ ○ ○ ○ ○ ○ ○ ○ ○ ○ (great)

Enjoyment: (poor) ○ ○ ○ ○ ○ ○ ○ ○ ○ ○ (great)

Notes/pics:

Ben More Assynt

Height: 998m

Date: ....

Ascent start time: .... Peak time: ....

Descent start time: .... Finish time: ....

Ascent duration: .... Descent duration: ....

Total time: [   ]

Total distance covered:...

Companions:...

....

....

Weather conditions:...

....

Difficulty: (poor) ○ ○ ○ ○ ○ ○ ○ ○ ○ ○ (great)

Views: (poor) ○ ○ ○ ○ ○ ○ ○ ○ ○ ○ (great)

Enjoyment: (poor) ○ ○ ○ ○ ○ ○ ○ ○ ○ ○ (great)

Notes/pics:

Stob Ban (Mamores)

Height: 999m

Date: ....

Ascent start time: .... Peak time: ....

Descent start time: .... Finish time: ....

Ascent duration: .... Descent duration: ....

Total time:

Total distance covered:...

Companions:..

....

....

Weather conditions:...

....

Difficulty: (poor) ○ ○ ○ ○ ○ ○ ○ ○ ○ ○ (great)

Views: (poor) ○ ○ ○ ○ ○ ○ ○ ○ ○ ○ (great)

Enjoyment: (poor) ○ ○ ○ ○ ○ ○ ○ ○ ○ ○ (great)

Notes/pics:

Sgurr Choinnich

Height: 999m

Date: ....

Ascent start time: .... Peak time: ....

Descent start time: .... Finish time: ....

Ascent duration: .... Descent duration: ....

Total time: [ ]

Total distance covered:...

Companions:...

....

....

Weather conditions:...

....

Difficulty: (poor) ○ ○ ○ ○ ○ ○ ○ ○ ○ ○ (great)

Views: (poor) ○ ○ ○ ○ ○ ○ ○ ○ ○ ○ (great)

Enjoyment: (poor) ○ ○ ○ ○ ○ ○ ○ ○ ○ ○ (great)

Notes/pics:

Sgurr Breac

Height: 999m

Date: ....

Ascent start time: .... Peak time: ....

Descent start time: .... Finish time: ....

Ascent duration: .... Descent duration: ....

Total time: [   ]

Total distance covered:...

Companions:...

....

....

Weather conditions:..

....

Difficulty: (poor) ○ ○ ○ ○ ○ ○ ○ ○ ○ (great)

Views: (poor) ○ ○ ○ ○ ○ ○ ○ ○ ○ (great)

Enjoyment: (poor) ○ ○ ○ ○ ○ ○ ○ ○ ○ (great)

Notes/pics:

Sgorr Dhonuill
(Beinn a'Bheithir)

Height: 1001m

Date: ....

Ascent start time: .... Peak time: ....

Descent start time: .... Finish time: ....

Ascent duration: .... Descent duration: ....

Total time:

Total distance covered:...

Companions:..

....

....

Weather conditions:...

....

Difficulty: (poor) ○ ○ ○ ○ ○ ○ ○ ○ ○ ○ (great)

Views: (poor) ○ ○ ○ ○ ○ ○ ○ ○ ○ ○ (great)

Enjoyment: (poor) ○ ○ ○ ○ ○ ○ ○ ○ ○ ○ (great)

Notes/pics:

Meall Greigh

Height: 1001m

Date: ....

Ascent start time: .... Peak time: ....

Descent start time: .... Finish time: ....

Ascent duration: .... Descent duration: ....

Total time: [   ]

Total distance covered:..

Companions:..

....

....

Weather conditions:..

....

Difficulty: (poor) ○ ○ ○ ○ ○ ○ ○ ○ ○ ○ (great)

Views: (poor) ○ ○ ○ ○ ○ ○ ○ ○ ○ ○ (great)

Enjoyment: (poor) ○ ○ ○ ○ ○ ○ ○ ○ ○ ○ (great)

Notes/pics:

Aonach Meadhoin

Height: 1001m

Date: ....

Ascent start time: .... Peak time: ....

Descent start time: .... Finish time: ....

Ascent duration: .... Descent duration: ....

Total time:

Total distance covered:...

Companions:...

....

....

Weather conditions:..

....

Difficulty: (poor) O O O O O O O O O (great)

Views: (poor) O O O O O O O O O (great)

Enjoyment: (poor) O O O O O O O O O (great)

Notes/pics:

Sgurr na Carnach

Height: 1002m

Date: ....

Ascent start time: .... Peak time: ....

Descent start time: .... Finish time: ....

Ascent duration: .... Descent duration: ....

Total time:

Total distance covered:...

Companions:...

....

....

Weather conditions:...

....

Difficulty: (poor) ○ ○ ○ ○ ○ ○ ○ ○ ○ ○ (great)

Views: (poor) ○ ○ ○ ○ ○ ○ ○ ○ ○ ○ (great)

Enjoyment: (poor) ○ ○ ○ ○ ○ ○ ○ ○ ○ ○ (great)

Notes/pics:

Sail Chaorainn

Height: 1002m

Date: ....

Ascent start time: .... Peak time: ....

Descent start time: .... Finish time: ....

Ascent duration: .... Descent duration: ....

Total time: [   ]

Total distance covered:...

Companions:...

....

....

Weather conditions:...

....

Difficulty:　(poor) ○ ○ ○ ○ ○ ○ ○ ○ ○ ○ (great)

Views:　(poor) ○ ○ ○ ○ ○ ○ ○ ○ ○ ○ (great)

Enjoyment: (poor) ○ ○ ○ ○ ○ ○ ○ ○ ○ ○ (great)

Notes/pics:

Sgurr Mor
(Loch Quoich)

Height: 1003m

Date: ....

Ascent start time: .... Peak time: ....

Descent start time: .... Finish time: ....

Ascent duration: .... Descent duration: ....

Total time:

Total distance covered: ....

Companions: ....

....

....

Weather conditions: ....

....

Difficulty: (poor) ○ ○ ○ ○ ○ ○ ○ ○ ○ ○ (great)

Views: (poor) ○ ○ ○ ○ ○ ○ ○ ○ ○ ○ (great)

Enjoyment: (poor) ○ ○ ○ ○ ○ ○ ○ ○ ○ ○ (great)

Notes/pics:

The Devil's Point

Height: 1004m

Date: ....

Ascent start time: .... Peak time: ....

Descent start time: .... Finish time: ....

Ascent duration: .... Descent duration: ....

Total time:

Total distance covered:..

Companions:..

....

....

Weather conditions:..

....

Difficulty: (poor) ○ ○ ○ ○ ○ ○ ○ ○ ○ ○ (great)

Views: (poor) ○ ○ ○ ○ ○ ○ ○ ○ ○ ○ (great)

Enjoyment: (poor) ○ ○ ○ ○ ○ ○ ○ ○ ○ ○ (great)

Notes/pics:

Sgurr an Lochain

Height: 1004m

Date: ....

Ascent start time: .... Peak time: ....

Descent start time: .... Finish time: ....

Ascent duration: .... Descent duration: ....

Total time: [   ]

Total distance covered: ....

Companions: ....

....

....

Weather conditions: ....

....

Difficulty: (poor) ○ ○ ○ ○ ○ ○ ○ ○ ○ ○ (great)

Views: (poor) ○ ○ ○ ○ ○ ○ ○ ○ ○ ○ (great)

Enjoyment: (poor) ○ ○ ○ ○ ○ ○ ○ ○ ○ ○ (great)

Notes/pics:

Beinn an Dothaidh

Height: 1004m

Date: ....

Ascent start time: .... Peak time: ....

Descent start time: .... Finish time: ....

Ascent duration: .... Descent duration: ....

Total time: [   ]

Total distance covered:...

Companions:...

....

....

Weather conditions:...

....

Difficulty: (poor) ○ ○ ○ ○ ○ ○ ○ ○ ○ (great)

Views: (poor) ○ ○ ○ ○ ○ ○ ○ ○ ○ (great)

Enjoyment: (poor) ○ ○ ○ ○ ○ ○ ○ ○ ○ (great)

Notes/pics:

Beinn Fhionnlaidh
(Carn Eige)

Height: 1005m

Date: ....

Ascent start time: .... Peak time: ....

Descent start time: .... Finish time: ....

Ascent duration: .... Descent duration: ....

Total time: [   ]

Total distance covered:...

Companions:..

....

....

Weather conditions:...

....

Difficulty: (poor) ○ ○ ○ ○ ○ ○ ○ ○ ○ ○ (great)

Views: (poor) ○ ○ ○ ○ ○ ○ ○ ○ ○ ○ (great)

Enjoyment: (poor) ○ ○ ○ ○ ○ ○ ○ ○ ○ ○ (great)

Notes/pics:

Carn Liath
(Creag Meagaidh)

Height: 1006m

Date: ....

Ascent start time: .... Peak time: ....

Descent start time: .... Finish time: ....

Ascent duration: .... Descent duration: ....

Total time: [   ]

Total distance covered:...

Companions:...

....

....

Weather conditions:...

....

Difficulty: (poor) O O O O O O O O O O (great)

Views: (poor) O O O O O O O O O O (great)

Enjoyment: (poor) O O O O O O O O O O (great)

Notes/pics:

An Sgarsoch

Height: 1006m

Date: ....

Ascent start time: .... Peak time: ....

Descent start time: .... Finish time: ....

Ascent duration: .... Descent duration: ....

Total time: [   ]

Total distance covered:...

Companions:..

....

....

Weather conditions:..

....

Difficulty: (poor) ○ ○ ○ ○ ○ ○ ○ ○ ○ ○ (great)

Views: (poor) ○ ○ ○ ○ ○ ○ ○ ○ ○ ○ (great)

Enjoyment: (poor) ○ ○ ○ ○ ○ ○ ○ ○ ○ ○ (great)

Notes/pics:

Maoile Lunndaidh

Height: 1007m

Date: ....

Ascent start time: .... Peak time: ....

Descent start time: .... Finish time: ....

Ascent duration: .... Descent duration: ....

Total time: [   ]

Total distance covered:..

Companions:..

....

....

Weather conditions:..

....

Difficulty: (poor) ○ ○ ○ ○ ○ ○ ○ ○ ○ ○ (great)

Views: (poor) ○ ○ ○ ○ ○ ○ ○ ○ ○ ○ (great)

Enjoyment: (poor) ○ ○ ○ ○ ○ ○ ○ ○ ○ ○ (great)

Notes/pics:

Beinn Dearg
(Blair Atholl)
Height: 1008m

Date: ....

Ascent start time: .... Peak time: ....

Descent start time: .... Finish time: ....

Ascent duration: .... Descent duration: ....

Total time:

Total distance covered:..

Companions:..

....

....

Weather conditions:...

....

Difficulty: (poor) ○ ○ ○ ○ ○ ○ ○ ○ ○ ○ (great)

Views: (poor) ○ ○ ○ ○ ○ ○ ○ ○ ○ ○ (great)

Enjoyment: (poor) ○ ○ ○ ○ ○ ○ ○ ○ ○ ○ (great)

Notes/pics:

The Saddle

Height: 1010m

Date: ....
Ascent start time: .... Peak time: ....
Descent start time: .... Finish time: ....

Ascent duration: .... Descent duration: ....

Total time: [   ]

Total distance covered:...

Companions:...

....

....

Weather conditions:...

....

Difficulty: (poor) ○ ○ ○ ○ ○ ○ ○ ○ ○ ○ (great)

Views: (poor) ○ ○ ○ ○ ○ ○ ○ ○ ○ ○ (great)

Enjoyment: (poor) ○ ○ ○ ○ ○ ○ ○ ○ ○ ○ (great)

Notes/pics:

Sgurr Eilde Mor

Height: 1010m

Date: ....

Ascent start time: .... Peak time: ....

Descent start time: .... Finish time: ....

Ascent duration: .... Descent duration: ....

Total time:

Total distance covered:...

Companions:...

....

....

Weather conditions:..

....

Difficulty: (poor) ○ ○ ○ ○ ○ ○ ○ ○ ○ ○ (great)

Views: (poor) ○ ○ ○ ○ ○ ○ ○ ○ ○ ○ (great)

Enjoyment: (poor) ○ ○ ○ ○ ○ ○ ○ ○ ○ ○ (great)

Notes/pics:

Sgurr an Doire Leathain

Height: 1010m

Date: ....

Ascent start time: .... Peak time: ....

Descent start time: .... Finish time: ....

Ascent duration: .... Descent duration: ....

Total time:

Total distance covered:..

Companions:..

....

....

Weather conditions:..

....

Difficulty: (poor) ○ ○ ○ ○ ○ ○ ○ ○ ○ ○ (great)

Views: (poor) ○ ○ ○ ○ ○ ○ ○ ○ ○ ○ (great)

Enjoyment: (poor) ○ ○ ○ ○ ○ ○ ○ ○ ○ ○ (great)

Notes/pics:

Ruadh-stac Mor
(Beinn Eighe)

Height: 1010m

Date: ....

Ascent start time: .... Peak time: ....

Descent start time: .... Finish time: ....

Ascent duration: .... Descent duration: ....

Total time: [   ]

Total distance covered:..

Companions:...

....

....

Weather conditions:...

....

Difficulty: (poor) ○ ○ ○ ○ ○ ○ ○ ○ ○ ○ (great)

Views: (poor) ○ ○ ○ ○ ○ ○ ○ ○ ○ ○ (great)

Enjoyment: (poor) ○ ○ ○ ○ ○ ○ ○ ○ ○ ○ (great)

Notes/pics:

Beinn Udlamain

Height: 1010m

Date: ....

Ascent start time: .... Peak time: ....

Descent start time: .... Finish time: ....

Ascent duration: .... Descent duration: ....

Total time:

Total distance covered:...

Companions:..

....

....

Weather conditions:..

....

Difficulty: (poor) ○ ○ ○ ○ ○ ○ ○ ○ ○ (great)

Views: (poor) ○ ○ ○ ○ ○ ○ ○ ○ ○ ○ (great)

Enjoyment: (poor) ○ ○ ○ ○ ○ ○ ○ ○ ○ (great)

Notes/pics:

Beinn Ime

Height: 1011m

Date: ....

Ascent start time: .... Peak time: ....

Descent start time: .... Finish time: ....

Ascent duration: .... Descent duration: ....

Total time: [ ]

Total distance covered: ....

Companions: ....

....

....

Weather conditions: ....

....

Difficulty: (poor) ○ ○ ○ ○ ○ ○ ○ ○ ○ (great)

Views: (poor) ○ ○ ○ ○ ○ ○ ○ ○ ○ (great)

Enjoyment: (poor) ○ ○ ○ ○ ○ ○ ○ ○ ○ (great)

Notes/pics:

Cairn Bannoch

Height: 1012m

Date: ....

Ascent start time: .... Peak time: ....

Descent start time: .... Finish time: ....

Ascent duration: .... Descent duration: ....

Total time:

Total distance covered:...

Companions:...

....

....

Weather conditions:...

....

Difficulty: (poor) ○ ○ ○ ○ ○ ○ ○ ○ ○ ○ (great)

Views: (poor) ○ ○ ○ ○ ○ ○ ○ ○ ○ ○ (great)

Enjoyment: (poor) ○ ○ ○ ○ ○ ○ ○ ○ ○ ○ (great)

Notes/pics:

Garbh Chioch Mhor

Height: 1013m

Date: ....

Ascent start time: .... Peak time: ....

Descent start time: .... Finish time: ....

Ascent duration: .... Descent duration: ....

Total time:

Total distance covered:...

Companions:...

....

....

Weather conditions:...

....

Difficulty: (poor) ○ ○ ○ ○ ○ ○ ○ ○ ○ (great)

Views: (poor) ○ ○ ○ ○ ○ ○ ○ ○ ○ (great)

Enjoyment: (poor) ○ ○ ○ ○ ○ ○ ○ ○ ○ (great)

Notes/pics:

Mullach Coire Mhic Fhearchair

Height: 1019m

Date: ....

Ascent start time: .... Peak time: ....

Descent start time: .... Finish time: ....

Ascent duration: .... Descent duration: ....

Total time:

Total distance covered:...

Companions:...

....

....

Weather conditions:...

....

Difficulty: (poor) ○ ○ ○ ○ ○ ○ ○ ○ ○ ○ (great)

Views: (poor) ○ ○ ○ ○ ○ ○ ○ ○ ○ ○ (great)

Enjoyment: (poor) ○ ○ ○ ○ ○ ○ ○ ○ ○ ○ (great)

Notes/pics:

Mullach Clach a'Bhlair

Height: 1019m

Date: ....

Ascent start time: .... Peak time: ....

Descent start time: .... Finish time: ....

Ascent duration: .... Descent duration: ....

Total time:

Total distance covered:...

Companions:..

....

....

Weather conditions:..

....

Difficulty: (poor) ○ ○ ○ ○ ○ ○ ○ ○ ○ ○ (great)

Views: (poor) ○ ○ ○ ○ ○ ○ ○ ○ ○ ○ (great)

Enjoyment: (poor) ○ ○ ○ ○ ○ ○ ○ ○ ○ ○ (great)

Notes/pics:

Carn an Tuirc

Height: 1019m

Date: ....

Ascent start time: .... Peak time: ....

Descent start time: .... Finish time: ....

Ascent duration: .... Descent duration: ....

Total time: [   ]

Total distance covered:...

Companions:...

....

....

Weather conditions:...

....

Difficulty: (poor) ○ ○ ○ ○ ○ ○ ○ ○ ○ (great)

Views: (poor) ○ ○ ○ ○ ○ ○ ○ ○ ○ (great)

Enjoyment: (poor) ○ ○ ○ ○ ○ ○ ○ ○ ○ (great)

Notes/pics:

Beinn Bheoil

Height: 1019m

Date: ....

Ascent start time: .... Peak time: ....

Descent start time: .... Finish time: ....

Ascent duration: .... Descent duration: ....

Total time:

Total distance covered:...

Companions:...

....

....

Weather conditions:..

....

Difficulty: (poor) ○ ○ ○ ○ ○ ○ ○ ○ ○ ○ (great)

Views: (poor) ○ ○ ○ ○ ○ ○ ○ ○ ○ ○ (great)

Enjoyment: (poor) ○ ○ ○ ○ ○ ○ ○ ○ ○ ○ (great)

Notes/pics:

Ladhar Bheinn

Height: 1020m

Date: ....

Ascent start time: .... Peak time: ....

Descent start time: .... Finish time: ....

Ascent duration: .... Descent duration: ....

Total time: [   ]

Total distance covered:...

Companions:...

....

....

Weather conditions:...

....

Difficulty: (poor) ○ ○ ○ ○ ○ ○ ○ ○ ○ (great)

Views: (poor) ○ ○ ○ ○ ○ ○ ○ ○ ○ (great)

Enjoyment: (poor) ○ ○ ○ ○ ○ ○ ○ ○ ○ (great)

Notes/pics:

Stob Dearg
(Buachaille Etive Mor)

Height: 1021m

Date: ....

Ascent start time: .... Peak time: ....

Descent start time: .... Finish time: ....

Ascent duration: .... Descent duration: ....

Total time:

Total distance covered:..

Companions:..

....

....

Weather conditions:..

....

Difficulty: (poor) ○ ○ ○ ○ ○ ○ ○ ○ ○ ○ (great)

Views: (poor) ○ ○ ○ ○ ○ ○ ○ ○ ○ ○ (great)

Enjoyment: (poor) ○ ○ ○ ○ ○ ○ ○ ○ ○ ○ (great)

Notes/pics:

Aonach Air Chrith

Height: 1021m

Date: ....
Ascent start time: .... Peak time: ....
Descent start time: .... Finish time: ....

Ascent duration: .... Descent duration: ....

Total time: [   ]

Total distance covered:...

Companions:...

....

....

Weather conditions:..

....

Difficulty: (poor) ○ ○ ○ ○ ○ ○ ○ ○ ○ (great)

Views: (poor) ○ ○ ○ ○ ○ ○ ○ ○ ○ (great)

Enjoyment: (poor) ○ ○ ○ ○ ○ ○ ○ ○ ○ (great)

Notes/pics:

Mullach an Rathain
(Liathach)

Height: 1023m

Date: ....

Ascent start time: .... Peak time: ....

Descent start time: .... Finish time: ....

Ascent duration: .... Descent duration: ....

Total time:

Total distance covered:...

Companions:...

....

....

Weather conditions:..

....

Difficulty: (poor) ○ ○ ○ ○ ○ ○ ○ ○ ○ ○ (great)

Views: (poor) ○ ○ ○ ○ ○ ○ ○ ○ ○ ○ (great)

Enjoyment: (poor) ○ ○ ○ ○ ○ ○ ○ ○ ○ ○ (great)

Notes/pics:

Sgorr Dhearg
(Beinn a'Bheithir)

Height: 1024m

Date: ....

Ascent start time: .... Peak time: ....

Descent start time: .... Finish time: ....

Ascent duration: .... Descent duration: ....

Total time: [   ]

Total distance covered:...

Companions:..

....

....

Weather conditions:..

....

Difficulty: (poor) ○ ○ ○ ○ ○ ○ ○ ○ ○ ○ (great)

Views: (poor) ○ ○ ○ ○ ○ ○ ○ ○ ○ ○ (great)

Enjoyment: (poor) ○ ○ ○ ○ ○ ○ ○ ○ ○ ○ (great)

Notes/pics:

Ben Challum

Height: 1025m

Date: ....

Ascent start time: .... Peak time: ....

Descent start time: .... Finish time: ....

Ascent duration: .... Descent duration: ....

Total time: [   ]

Total distance covered:..

Companions:...

....

....

Weather conditions:...

....

Difficulty: (poor) ○ ○ ○ ○ ○ ○ ○ ○ ○ (great)

Views: (poor) ○ ○ ○ ○ ○ ○ ○ ○ ○ (great)

Enjoyment: (poor) ○ ○ ○ ○ ○ ○ ○ ○ ○ (great)

Notes/pics:

Sgurr na Ciste Duibhe

Height: 1027m

Date: ....

Ascent start time: .... Peak time: ....

Descent start time: .... Finish time: ....

Ascent duration: .... Descent duration: ....

Total time: [   ]

Total distance covered:...

Companions:...

....

....

Weather conditions:..

....

Difficulty: (poor) ○ ○ ○ ○ ○ ○ ○ ○ ○ ○ (great)

Views: (poor) ○ ○ ○ ○ ○ ○ ○ ○ ○ ○ (great)

Enjoyment: (poor) ○ ○ ○ ○ ○ ○ ○ ○ ○ ○ (great)

Notes/pics:

Sgurr a'Mhaoraich

Height: 1027m

Date: ....

Ascent start time: .... Peak time: ....

Descent start time: .... Finish time: ....

Ascent duration: .... Descent duration: ....

Total time:

Total distance covered:..

Companions:..

....

....

Weather conditions:..

....

Difficulty: (poor) ○ ○ ○ ○ ○ ○ ○ ○ ○ ○ (great)

Views: (poor) ○ ○ ○ ○ ○ ○ ○ ○ ○ ○ (great)

Enjoyment: (poor) ○ ○ ○ ○ ○ ○ ○ ○ ○ ○ (great)

Notes/pics:

Carn Gorm

Height: 1029m

Date: ....
Ascent start time: .... Peak time: ....
Descent start time: .... Finish time: ....

Ascent duration: .... Descent duration: ....

Total time: [   ]

Total distance covered:..

Companions:..

....

....

Weather conditions:..

....

Difficulty: (poor) ○ ○ ○ ○ ○ ○ ○ ○ ○ ○ (great)

Views: (poor) ○ ○ ○ ○ ○ ○ ○ ○ ○ ○ (great)

Enjoyment: (poor) ○ ○ ○ ○ ○ ○ ○ ○ ○ ○ (great)

Notes/pics:

Carn an Righ

Height: 1029m

Date: ....

Ascent start time: .... Peak time: ....

Descent start time: .... Finish time: ....

Ascent duration: .... Descent duration: ....

Total time: [   ]

Total distance covered:...

Companions:...

....

....

Weather conditions:..

....

Difficulty: (poor) ○ ○ ○ ○ ○ ○ ○ ○ ○ ○ (great)

Views: (poor) ○ ○ ○ ○ ○ ○ ○ ○ ○ ○ (great)

Enjoyment: (poor) ○ ○ ○ ○ ○ ○ ○ ○ ○ ○ (great)

Notes/pics:

Ben Oss

Height: 1029m

Date: ....

Ascent start time: .... Peak time: ....

Descent start time: .... Finish time: ....

Ascent duration: .... Descent duration: ....

Total time:

Total distance covered:...

Companions:..

....

....

Weather conditions:...

....

Difficulty: (poor) ○ ○ ○ ○ ○ ○ ○ ○ ○ (great)

Views: (poor) ○ ○ ○ ○ ○ ○ ○ ○ ○ (great)

Enjoyment: (poor) ○ ○ ○ ○ ○ ○ ○ ○ ○ (great)

Notes/pics:

Beinn Fhada

Height: 1032m

Date: ....

Ascent start time: .... Peak time: ....

Descent start time: .... Finish time: ....

Ascent duration: .... Descent duration: ....

Total time: [   ]

Total distance covered:...

Companions:...

....

....

Weather conditions:...

....

Difficulty: (poor) ○ ○ ○ ○ ○ ○ ○ ○ ○ ○ (great)

Views: (poor) ○ ○ ○ ○ ○ ○ ○ ○ ○ ○ (great)

Enjoyment: (poor) ○ ○ ○ ○ ○ ○ ○ ○ ○ ○ (great)

Notes/pics:

Am Bodach

Height: 1032m

Date: ....

Ascent start time: .... Peak time: ....

Descent start time: .... Finish time: ....

Ascent duration: .... Descent duration: ....

Total time: [   ]

Total distance covered:...

Companions:...

....

....

Weather conditions:...

....

Difficulty: (poor) ○ ○ ○ ○ ○ ○ ○ ○ ○ ○ (great)

Views: (poor) ○ ○ ○ ○ ○ ○ ○ ○ ○ ○ (great)

Enjoyment: (poor) ○ ○ ○ ○ ○ ○ ○ ○ ○ ○ (great)

Notes/pics:

Carn Dearg
(Loch Pattack)

Height: 1034m

Date: ....

Ascent start time: .... Peak time: ....

Descent start time: .... Finish time: ....

Ascent duration: .... Descent duration: ....

Total time: [   ]

Total distance covered:..

Companions:...

....

....

Weather conditions:..

....

Difficulty: (poor) ○ ○ ○ ○ ○ ○ ○ ○ ○ ○ (great)

Views: (poor) ○ ○ ○ ○ ○ ○ ○ ○ ○ ○ (great)

Enjoyment: (poor) ○ ○ ○ ○ ○ ○ ○ ○ ○ ○ (great)

Notes/pics:

Gleouraich

Height: 1035m

Date: ....

Ascent start time: .... Peak time: ....

Descent start time: .... Finish time: ....

Ascent duration: .... Descent duration: ....

Total time: [   ]

Total distance covered: ....

Companions: ....

....

....

Weather conditions: ....

....

Difficulty: (poor) ○ ○ ○ ○ ○ ○ ○ ○ ○ ○ (great)

Views: (poor) ○ ○ ○ ○ ○ ○ ○ ○ ○ ○ (great)

Enjoyment: (poor) ○ ○ ○ ○ ○ ○ ○ ○ ○ ○ (great)

Notes/pics:

Sgurr a'Bhealaich Dheirg

Height: 1036m

Date: ....

Ascent start time: .... Peak time: ....

Descent start time: .... Finish time: ....

Ascent duration: .... Descent duration: ....

Total time:

Total distance covered:...

Companions:...

....

....

Weather conditions:...

....

Difficulty: (poor) ○ ○ ○ ○ ○ ○ ○ ○ ○ ○ (great)

Views: (poor) ○ ○ ○ ○ ○ ○ ○ ○ ○ ○ (great)

Enjoyment: (poor) ○ ○ ○ ○ ○ ○ ○ ○ ○ ○ (great)

Notes/pics:

Carn a'Mhaim

Height: 1037m

Date: ....
Ascent start time: .... Peak time: ....
Descent start time: .... Finish time: ....

Ascent duration: .... Descent duration: ....

Total time: [   ]

Total distance covered:...

Companions:..

....

....

Weather conditions:...

....

Difficulty: (poor) ○ ○ ○ ○ ○ ○ ○ ○ ○ ○ (great)

Views: (poor) ○ ○ ○ ○ ○ ○ ○ ○ ○ ○ (great)

Enjoyment: (poor) ○ ○ ○ ○ ○ ○ ○ ○ ○ ○ (great)

Notes/pics:

Beinn Achaladair

Height: 1038m

Date: ....

Ascent start time: .... Peak time: ....

Descent start time: .... Finish time: ....

Ascent duration: .... Descent duration: ....

Total time:

Total distance covered:...

Companions:...

....

....

Weather conditions:...

....

Difficulty: (poor) ○ ○ ○ ○ ○ ○ ○ ○ ○ ○ (great)

Views: (poor) ○ ○ ○ ○ ○ ○ ○ ○ ○ ○ (great)

Enjoyment: (poor) ○ ○ ○ ○ ○ ○ ○ ○ ○ ○ (great)

Notes/pics:

Meall Ghaordaidh

Height: 1039m

Date: ....

Ascent start time: .... Peak time: ....

Descent start time: .... Finish time: ....

Ascent duration: .... Descent duration: ....

Total time: [ ]

Total distance covered:...

Companions:..

....

....

Weather conditions:...

....

Difficulty: (poor) ○ ○ ○ ○ ○ ○ ○ ○ ○ ○ (great)

Views: (poor) ○ ○ ○ ○ ○ ○ ○ ○ ○ ○ (great)

Enjoyment: (poor) ○ ○ ○ ○ ○ ○ ○ ○ ○ ○ (great)

Notes/pics:

Sgurr na Ciche

Height: 1040m

Date: ....

Ascent start time: .... Peak time: ....

Descent start time: .... Finish time: ....

Ascent duration: .... Descent duration: ....

Total time: [   ]

Total distance covered:..

Companions:...

....

....

Weather conditions:..

....

Difficulty: (poor) ○ ○ ○ ○ ○ ○ ○ ○ ○ ○ (great)

Views: (poor) ○ ○ ○ ○ ○ ○ ○ ○ ○ ○ (great)

Enjoyment: (poor) ○ ○ ○ ○ ○ ○ ○ ○ ○ ○ (great)

Notes/pics:

Carn Mairg

Height: 1042m

Date: ....
Ascent start time: .... Peak time: ....
Descent start time: .... Finish time: ....

Ascent duration: .... Descent duration: ....

Total time: [ ]

Total distance covered:..

Companions:..

....

....

Weather conditions:..

....

Difficulty: (poor) ○ ○ ○ ○ ○ ○ ○ ○ ○ (great)

Views: (poor) ○ ○ ○ ○ ○ ○ ○ ○ ○ (great)

Enjoyment: (poor) ○ ○ ○ ○ ○ ○ ○ ○ ○ (great)

Notes/pics:

Stob Coir an Albannaich

Height: 1044m

Date: ....

Ascent start time: .... Peak time: ....

Descent start time: .... Finish time: ....

Ascent duration: .... Descent duration: ....

Total time: [   ]

Total distance covered:..

Companions:...

....

....

Weather conditions:..

....

Difficulty: (poor) ○ ○ ○ ○ ○ ○ ○ ○ ○ ○ (great)

Views: (poor) ○ ○ ○ ○ ○ ○ ○ ○ ○ ○ (great)

Enjoyment: (poor) ○ ○ ○ ○ ○ ○ ○ ○ ○ ○ (great)

Notes/pics:

Meall nan Tarmachan

Height: 1044m

Date: ....

Ascent start time: .... Peak time: ....

Descent start time: .... Finish time: ....

Ascent duration: .... Descent duration: ....

Total time: [   ]

Total distance covered:...

Companions:..

....

....

Weather conditions:..

....

Difficulty: (poor) ○ ○ ○ ○ ○ ○ ○ ○ ○ ○ (great)

Views: (poor) ○ ○ ○ ○ ○ ○ ○ ○ ○ ○ (great)

Enjoyment: (poor) ○ ○ ○ ○ ○ ○ ○ ○ ○ ○ (great)

Notes/pics:

Beinn Iutharn Mhor

Height: 1045m

Date: ....

Ascent start time: .... Peak time: ....

Descent start time: .... Finish time: ....

Ascent duration: .... Descent duration: ....

Total time:

Total distance covered:...

Companions:...

....

....

Weather conditions:...

....

Difficulty: (poor) O O O O O O O O O O (great)

Views: (poor) O O O O O O O O O O (great)

Enjoyment: (poor) O O O O O O O O O O (great)

Notes/pics:

Cruach Ardrain

Height: 1046m

Date: ....

Ascent start time: .... Peak time: ....

Descent start time: .... Finish time: ....

Ascent duration: .... Descent duration: ....

Total time: [   ]

Total distance covered:...

Companions:...

....

....

Weather conditions:..

....

Difficulty: (poor) ○ ○ ○ ○ ○ ○ ○ ○ ○ ○ (great)

Views: (poor) ○ ○ ○ ○ ○ ○ ○ ○ ○ ○ (great)

Enjoyment: (poor) ○ ○ ○ ○ ○ ○ ○ ○ ○ ○ (great)

Notes/pics:

Chno Dearg

Height: 1046m

Date: ....

Ascent start time: .... Peak time: ....

Descent start time: .... Finish time: ....

Ascent duration: .... Descent duration: ....

Total time:

Total distance covered:...

Companions:..

....

....

Weather conditions:...

....

Difficulty: (poor) ⭘⭘⭘⭘⭘⭘⭘⭘⭘⭘ (great)

Views: (poor) ⭘⭘⭘⭘⭘⭘⭘⭘⭘⭘ (great)

Enjoyment: (poor) ⭘⭘⭘⭘⭘⭘⭘⭘⭘⭘ (great)

Notes/pics:

Ben Wyvis

Height: 1046m

Date: ....

Ascent start time: .... Peak time: ....

Descent start time: .... Finish time: ....

Ascent duration: .... Descent duration: ....

Total time: [   ]

Total distance covered: ....

Companions: ....

....

....

Weather conditions: ....

....

Difficulty: (poor) ○ ○ ○ ○ ○ ○ ○ ○ ○ ○ (great)

Views: (poor) ○ ○ ○ ○ ○ ○ ○ ○ ○ ○ (great)

Enjoyment: (poor) ○ ○ ○ ○ ○ ○ ○ ○ ○ ○ (great)

Notes/pics:

Creag Mhor
(Glen Lochay)

Height: 1047m

Date: ....

Ascent start time: .... Peak time: ....

Descent start time: .... Finish time: ....

Ascent duration: .... Descent duration: ....

Total time: [   ]

Total distance covered:..

Companions:..

....

....

Weather conditions:...

....

Difficulty: (poor) ○ ○ ○ ○ ○ ○ ○ ○ ○ (great)

Views: (poor) ○ ○ ○ ○ ○ ○ ○ ○ ○ (great)

Enjoyment: (poor) ○ ○ ○ ○ ○ ○ ○ ○ ○ (great)

Notes/pics:

Carn an t-Sagairt Mor

Height: 1047m

Date: ....

Ascent start time: .... Peak time: ....

Descent start time: .... Finish time: ....

Ascent duration: .... Descent duration: ....

Total time:

Total distance covered:...

Companions:...

....

....

Weather conditions:..

....

Difficulty: (poor) ○ ○ ○ ○ ○ ○ ○ ○ ○ ○ (great)

Views: (poor) ○ ○ ○ ○ ○ ○ ○ ○ ○ ○ (great)

Enjoyment: (poor) ○ ○ ○ ○ ○ ○ ○ ○ ○ ○ (great)

Notes/pics:

Sgurr Fhuar-thuill

Height: 1049m

Date: ....

Ascent start time: .... Peak time: ....

Descent start time: .... Finish time: ....

Ascent duration: .... Descent duration: ....

Total time:

Total distance covered:..

Companions:...

....

....

Weather conditions:...

....

Difficulty: (poor) O O O O O O O O O O (great)

Views: (poor) O O O O O O O O O O (great)

Enjoyment: (poor) O O O O O O O O O O (great)

Notes/pics:

Geal Charn

Height: 1049m

Date: ....

Ascent start time: .... Peak time: ....

Descent start time: .... Finish time: ....

Ascent duration: .... Descent duration: ....

Total time: [   ]

Total distance covered:...

Companions:...

....

....

Weather conditions:...

....

Difficulty: (poor) ○ ○ ○ ○ ○ ○ ○ ○ ○ (great)

Views: (poor) ○ ○ ○ ○ ○ ○ ○ ○ ○ (great)

Enjoyment: (poor) ○ ○ ○ ○ ○ ○ ○ ○ ○ (great)

Notes/pics:

Beinn a'Chaorainn
(Glen Spean)

Height: 1050m

Date: ....

Ascent start time: .... Peak time: ....

Descent start time: .... Finish time: ....

Ascent duration: .... Descent duration: ....

Total time: [   ]

Total distance covered: ....

Companions: ....

....

....

Weather conditions: ....

....

Difficulty: (poor) ○ ○ ○ ○ ○ ○ ○ ○ ○ (great)

Views: (poor) ○ ○ ○ ○ ○ ○ ○ ○ ○ (great)

Enjoyment: (poor) ○ ○ ○ ○ ○ ○ ○ ○ ○ (great)

Notes/pics:

Glas Tulaichean

Height: 1051m

Date: ....
Ascent start time: .... Peak time: ....
Descent start time: .... Finish time: ....

Ascent duration: .... Descent duration: ....

Total time:

Total distance covered:..

Companions:...

....

....

Weather conditions:..

....

Difficulty: (poor) ○ ○ ○ ○ ○ ○ ○ ○ ○ ○ (great)

Views: (poor) ○ ○ ○ ○ ○ ○ ○ ○ ○ ○ (great)

Enjoyment: (poor) ○ ○ ○ ○ ○ ○ ○ ○ ○ ○ (great)

Notes/pics:

Sgurr a'Chaorachain

Height: 1053m

Date: ....

Ascent start time: .... Peak time: ....

Descent start time: .... Finish time: ....

Ascent duration: .... Descent duration: ....

Total time:

Total distance covered:..

Companions:..

....

....

Weather conditions:..

....

Difficulty: (poor) ○ ○ ○ ○ ○ ○ ○ ○ ○ (great)

Views: (poor) ○ ○ ○ ○ ○ ○ ○ ○ ○ (great)

Enjoyment: (poor) ○ ○ ○ ○ ○ ○ ○ ○ ○ (great)

Notes/pics:

Toll Creagach

Height: 1054m

Date: ....

Ascent start time: .... Peak time: ....

Descent start time: .... Finish time: ....

Ascent duration: .... Descent duration: ....

Total time:

Total distance covered:..

Companions:...

....

....

Weather conditions:..

....

Difficulty: (poor) ○ ○ ○ ○ ○ ○ ○ ○ ○ ○ (great)

Views: (poor) ○ ○ ○ ○ ○ ○ ○ ○ ○ ○ (great)

Enjoyment: (poor) ○ ○ ○ ○ ○ ○ ○ ○ ○ ○ (great)

Notes/pics:

Stob Poite Coire Ardair

Height: 1054m

Date: ....

Ascent start time: .... Peak time: ....

Descent start time: .... Finish time: ....

Ascent duration: .... Descent duration: ....

Total time: [   ]

Total distance covered: ....

Companions: ....

....

....

Weather conditions: ....

....

Difficulty: (poor) ○ ○ ○ ○ ○ ○ ○ ○ ○ ○ (great)

Views: . (poor) ○ ○ ○ ○ ○ ○ ○ ○ ○ ○ (great)

Enjoyment: (poor) ○ ○ ○ ○ ○ ○ ○ ○ ○ ○ (great)

Notes/pics:

Spidean a'Choire Leith (Liathach)

Height: 1055m

Date: ....

Ascent start time: .... Peak time: ....

Descent start time: .... Finish time: ....

Ascent duration: .... Descent duration: ....

Total time: [   ]

Total distance covered:...

Companions:...

....

....

Weather conditions:...

....

Difficulty: (poor) ○ ○ ○ ○ ○ ○ ○ ○ ○ (great)

Views: (poor) ○ ○ ○ ○ ○ ○ ○ ○ ○ (great)

Enjoyment: (poor) ○ ○ ○ ○ ○ ○ ○ ○ ○ (great)

Notes/pics:

Na Gruagaichean

Height: 1056m

Date: ....

Ascent start time: .... Peak time: ....

Descent start time: .... Finish time: ....

Ascent duration: .... Descent duration: ....

Total time:

Total distance covered:..

Companions:..

....

....

Weather conditions:...

....

Difficulty: (poor) ○ ○ ○ ○ ○ ○ ○ ○ ○ ○ (great)

Views: (poor) ○ ○ ○ ○ ○ ○ ○ ○ ○ ○ (great)

Enjoyment: (poor) ○ ○ ○ ○ ○ ○ ○ ○ ○ ○ (great)

Notes/pics:

Sgurr Fiona
(An Teallach)

Height: 1060m

Date: ....

Ascent start time: .... Peak time: ....

Descent start time: .... Finish time: ....

Ascent duration: .... Descent duration: ....

Total time:

Total distance covered:...

Companions:..

....

....

Weather conditions:...

....

Difficulty: (poor) ○ ○ ○ ○ ○ ○ ○ ○ ○ ○ (great)

Views: (poor) ○ ○ ○ ○ ○ ○ ○ ○ ○ ○ (great)

Enjoyment: (poor) ○ ○ ○ ○ ○ ○ ○ ○ ○ ○ (great)

Notes/pics:

Bidein a'Ghlas Thuill
(An Teallach)

Height: 1062m

Date: ....

Ascent start time: .... Peak time: ....

Descent start time: .... Finish time: ....

Ascent duration: .... Descent duration: ....

Total time: [   ]

Total distance covered:..

Companions:...

....

....

Weather conditions:..

....

Difficulty: (poor) ○ ○ ○ ○ ○ ○ ○ ○ ○ ○ (great)

Views: (poor) ○ ○ ○ ○ ○ ○ ○ ○ ○ ○ (great)

Enjoyment: (poor) ○ ○ ○ ○ ○ ○ ○ ○ ○ ○ (great)

Notes/pics:

Cairn of Claise

Height: 1064m

Date: ....

Ascent start time: .... Peak time: ....

Descent start time: .... Finish time: ....

Ascent duration: .... Descent duration: ....

Total time: [   ]

Total distance covered:...

Companions:...

....

....

Weather conditions:..

....

Difficulty: (poor) O O O O O O O O O O (great)

Views: (poor) O O O O O O O O O O (great)

Enjoyment: (poor) O O O O O O O O O O (great)

Notes/pics:

Sgurr Fhuaran

Height: 1067m

Date: ....

Ascent start time: .... Peak time: ....

Descent start time: .... Finish time: ....

Ascent duration: .... Descent duration: ....

Total time:

Total distance covered:...

Companions:...

....

....

Weather conditions:...

....

Difficulty: (poor) ○ ○ ○ ○ ○ ○ ○ ○ ○ ○ (great)

Views: (poor) ○ ○ ○ ○ ○ ○ ○ ○ ○ ○ (great)

Enjoyment: (poor) ○ ○ ○ ○ ○ ○ ○ ○ ○ ○ (great)

Notes/pics:

Glas Maol

Height: 1068m

Date: ....

Ascent start time: .... Peak time: ....

Descent start time: .... Finish time: ....

Ascent duration: .... Descent duration: ....

Total time: [   ]

Total distance covered:..

Companions:..

....

....

Weather conditions:...

....

Difficulty: (poor) ○ ○ ○ ○ ○ ○ ○ ○ ○ (great)

Views: (poor) ○ ○ ○ ○ ○ ○ ○ ○ ○ (great)

Enjoyment: (poor) ○ ○ ○ ○ ○ ○ ○ ○ ○ (great)

Notes/pics:

Meall Corranaich

Height: 1069m

Date: ....

Ascent start time: .... Peak time: ....

Descent start time: .... Finish time: ....

Ascent duration: .... Descent duration: ....

Total time: [ ]

Total distance covered: ....

Companions: ....

....

....

Weather conditions: ....

....

Difficulty: (poor) ○ ○ ○ ○ ○ ○ ○ ○ ○ ○ (great)

Views: (poor) ○ ○ ○ ○ ○ ○ ○ ○ ○ ○ (great)

Enjoyment: (poor) ○ ○ ○ ○ ○ ○ ○ ○ ○ ○ (great)

Notes/pics:

An Socach (Mullardoch)

Height: 1069m

Date: ....

Ascent start time: .... Peak time: ....

Descent start time: .... Finish time: ....

Ascent duration: .... Descent duration: ....

Total time: [   ]

Total distance covered:..

Companions:..

....

....

Weather conditions:..

....

Difficulty: (poor) ○ ○ ○ ○ ○ ○ ○ ○ ○ ○ (great)

Views: (poor) ○ ○ ○ ○ ○ ○ ○ ○ ○ ○ (great)

Enjoyment: (poor) ○ ○ ○ ○ ○ ○ ○ ○ ○ ○ (great)

Notes/pics:

Braigh Coire Chruinn-bhalgain

Height: 1070m

Date: ....

Ascent start time: .... Peak time: ....

Descent start time: .... Finish time: ....

Ascent duration: .... Descent duration: ....

Total time: [   ]

Total distance covered:...

Companions:...

....

....

Weather conditions:...

....

Difficulty: (poor) ○ ○ ○ ○ ○ ○ ○ ○ ○ ○ (great)

Views: (poor) ○ ○ ○ ○ ○ ○ ○ ○ ○ ○ (great)

Enjoyment: (poor) ○ ○ ○ ○ ○ ○ ○ ○ ○ ○ (great)

Notes/pics:

Stob Coire Sgreamhach

Height: 1072m

Date: ....

Ascent start time: .... Peak time: ....

Descent start time: .... Finish time: ....

Ascent duration: .... Descent duration: ....

Total time: [   ]

Total distance covered:...

Companions:...

....

....

Weather conditions:...

....

Difficulty: (poor) ○ ○ ○ ○ ○ ○ ○ ○ ○ ○ (great)

Views: (poor) ○ ○ ○ ○ ○ ○ ○ ○ ○ ○ (great)

Enjoyment: (poor) ○ ○ ○ ○ ○ ○ ○ ○ ○ ○ (great)

Notes/pics:

Beinn Dorain

Height: 1076m

Date: ....

Ascent start time: .... Peak time: ....

Descent start time: .... Finish time: ....

Ascent duration: .... Descent duration: ....

Total time:

Total distance covered:..

Companions:...

....

....

Weather conditions:..

....

Difficulty: (poor) ○ ○ ○ ○ ○ ○ ○ ○ ○ ○ (great)

Views: (poor) ○ ○ ○ ○ ○ ○ ○ ○ ○ ○ (great)

Enjoyment: (poor) ○ ○ ○ ○ ○ ○ ○ ○ ○ ○ (great)

Notes/pics:

Ben Starav

Height: 1078m

Date: ....

Ascent start time: .... Peak time: ....

Descent start time: .... Finish time: ....

Ascent duration: .... Descent duration: ....

Total time: [ ]

Total distance covered:...

Companions:...

....

....

Weather conditions:...

....

Difficulty: (poor) O O O O O O O O O O (great)

Views: (poor) O O O O O O O O O O (great)

Enjoyment: (poor) O O O O O O O O O O (great)

Notes/pics:

Beinn Heasgarnich

Height: 1078m

Date: ....

Ascent start time: .... Peak time: ....

Descent start time: .... Finish time: ....

Ascent duration: .... Descent duration: ....

Total time:

Total distance covered: ....

Companions: ....

....

....

Weather conditions: ....

....

Difficulty: (poor) ○ ○ ○ ○ ○ ○ ○ ○ ○ ○ (great)

Views: (poor) ○ ○ ○ ○ ○ ○ ○ ○ ○ ○ (great)

Enjoyment: (poor) ○ ○ ○ ○ ○ ○ ○ ○ ○ ○ (great)

Notes/pics:

Beinn a'Chreachain

Height: 1081m

Date: ....

Ascent start time: .... Peak time: ....

Descent start time: .... Finish time: ....

Ascent duration: .... Descent duration: ....

Total time: [   ]

Total distance covered:..

Companions:..

....

....

Weather conditions:..

....

Difficulty: (poor) ○ ○ ○ ○ ○ ○ ○ ○ ○ (great)

Views: (poor) ○ ○ ○ ○ ○ ○ ○ ○ ○ (great)

Enjoyment: (poor) ○ ○ ○ ○ ○ ○ ○ ○ ○ (great)

Notes/pics:

Beinn a'Chaorainn
(Cairngorms)

Height: 1082m

Date: ....

Ascent start time: .... Peak time: ....

Descent start time: .... Finish time: ....

Ascent duration: .... Descent duration: ....

Total time: [   ]

Total distance covered:...

Companions:...

....

....

Weather conditions:..

....

Difficulty: (poor) ○ ○ ○ ○ ○ ○ ○ ○ ○ (great)

Views: (poor) ○ ○ ○ ○ ○ ○ ○ ○ ○ (great)

Enjoyment: (poor) ○ ○ ○ ○ ○ ○ ○ ○ ○ (great)

Notes/pics:

Sgurr a'Choire Ghlais

Height: 1083m

Date: ....

Ascent start time: .... Peak time: ....

Descent start time: .... Finish time: ....

Ascent duration: .... Descent duration: ....

Total time: [   ]

Total distance covered:...

Companions:..

....

....

Weather conditions:...

....

Difficulty: (poor) ○ ○ ○ ○ ○ ○ ○ ○ ○ ○ (great)

Views: (poor) ○ ○ ○ ○ ○ ○ ○ ○ ○ ○ (great)

Enjoyment: (poor) ○ ○ ○ ○ ○ ○ ○ ○ ○ ○ (great)

Notes/pics:

Schiehallion

Height: 1083m

Date: ....

Ascent start time: .... Peak time: ....

Descent start time: .... Finish time: ....

Ascent duration: .... Descent duration: ....

Total time: [   ]

Total distance covered:...

Companions:...

....

....

Weather conditions:..

....

Difficulty:　(poor) ○ ○ ○ ○ ○ ○ ○ ○ ○ ○ (great)

Views:　(poor) ○ ○ ○ ○ ○ ○ ○ ○ ○ ○ (great)

Enjoyment: (poor) ○ ○ ○ ○ ○ ○ ○ ○ ○ ○ (great)

Notes/pics:

Beinn Dearg
(Ullapool)

Height: 1084m

Date: ....

Ascent start time: .... Peak time: ....

Descent start time: .... Finish time: ....

Ascent duration: .... Descent duration: ....

Total time: ⌈⎯⎯⎯⎯⎯⎯⎯⎯⎯⎯⎯⌉

Total distance covered:...

Companions:..

....

....

Weather conditions:...

....

Difficulty: (poor) ○ ○ ○ ○ ○ ○ ○ ○ ○ ○ (great)

Views: (poor) ○ ○ ○ ○ ○ ○ ○ ○ ○ ○ (great)

Enjoyment: (poor) ○ ○ ○ ○ ○ ○ ○ ○ ○ ○ (great)

Notes/pics:

Beinn a'Chlachair

Height: 1087m

Date: ....

Ascent start time: .... Peak time: ....

Descent start time: .... Finish time: ....

Ascent duration: .... Descent duration: ....

Total time:

Total distance covered: ....

Companions: ....

....

....

Weather conditions: ....

....

Difficulty: (poor) ○ ○ ○ ○ ○ ○ ○ ○ ○ (great)

Views: (poor) ○ ○ ○ ○ ○ ○ ○ ○ ○ (great)

Enjoyment: (poor) ○ ○ ○ ○ ○ ○ ○ ○ ○ (great)

Notes/pics:

Stob Ghabhar

Height: 1090m

Date: ....

Ascent start time: .... Peak time: ....

Descent start time: .... Finish time: ....

Ascent duration: .... Descent duration: ....

Total time: [   ]

Total distance covered:...

Companions:..

....

....

Weather conditions:..

....

Difficulty: (poor) ⭕⭕⭕⭕⭕⭕⭕⭕⭕ (great)

Views: (poor) ⭕⭕⭕⭕⭕⭕⭕⭕⭕ (great)

Enjoyment: (poor) ⭕⭕⭕⭕⭕⭕⭕⭕⭕ (great)

Notes/pics:

Bynack More

Height: 1090m

Date: ....

Ascent start time: .... Peak time: ....

Descent start time: .... Finish time: ....

Ascent duration: .... Descent duration: ....

Total time: [   ]

Total distance covered:...

Companions:...

....

....

Weather conditions:...

....

Difficulty: (poor) ○ ○ ○ ○ ○ ○ ○ ○ ○ ○ (great)

Views: (poor) ○ ○ ○ ○ ○ ○ ○ ○ ○ ○ (great)

Enjoyment: (poor) ○ ○ ○ ○ ○ ○ ○ ○ ○ ○ (great)

Notes/pics:

Sgurr nan Clach Geala

Height: 1093m

Date: ....

Ascent start time: .... Peak time: ....

Descent start time: .... Finish time: ....

Ascent duration: .... Descent duration: ....

Total time: [　　　　　　]

Total distance covered:...

Companions:...

....

....

Weather conditions:..

....

Difficulty: (poor) ○ ○ ○ ○ ○ ○ ○ ○ ○ ○ (great)

Views: (poor) ○ ○ ○ ○ ○ ○ ○ ○ ○ ○ (great)

Enjoyment: (poor) ○ ○ ○ ○ ○ ○ ○ ○ ○ ○ (great)

Notes/pics:

Sgurr Choinnich Mor

Height: 1094m

Date: ....

Ascent start time: .... Peak time: ....

Descent start time: .... Finish time: ....

Ascent duration: .... Descent duration: ....

Total time:

Total distance covered: ....

Companions: ....

....

....

Weather conditions: ....

....

Difficulty: (poor) ○ ○ ○ ○ ○ ○ ○ ○ ○ ○ (great)

Views: (poor) ○ ○ ○ ○ ○ ○ ○ ○ ○ ○ (great)

Enjoyment: (poor) ○ ○ ○ ○ ○ ○ ○ ○ ○ ○ (great)

Notes/pics:

Sgurr a'Mhaim

Height: 1099m

Date: ....

Ascent start time: .... Peak time: ....

Descent start time: .... Finish time: ....

Ascent duration: .... Descent duration: ....

Total time: [   ]

Total distance covered:..

Companions:..

....

....

Weather conditions:..

....

Difficulty: (poor) ○ ○ ○ ○ ○ ○ ○ ○ ○ ○ (great)

Views: (poor) ○ ○ ○ ○ ○ ○ ○ ○ ○ ○ (great)

Enjoyment: (poor) ○ ○ ○ ○ ○ ○ ○ ○ ○ ○ (great)

Notes/pics:

Creise

Height: 1100m

Date: ....

Ascent start time: .... Peak time: ....

Descent start time: .... Finish time: ....

Ascent duration: .... Descent duration: ....

Total time: [ ]

Total distance covered:...

Companions:..

....

....

Weather conditions:...

....

Difficulty: (poor) ○ ○ ○ ○ ○ ○ ○ ○ ○ (great)

Views: (poor) ○ ○ ○ ○ ○ ○ ○ ○ ○ (great)

Enjoyment: (poor) ○ ○ ○ ○ ○ ○ ○ ○ ○ (great)

Notes/pics:

Mullach Fraoch-choire

Height: 1102m

Date: ....

Ascent start time: .... Peak time: ....

Descent start time: .... Finish time: ....

Ascent duration: .... Descent duration: ....

Total time: [   ]

Total distance covered:..

Companions:...

....

....

Weather conditions:...

....

Difficulty: (poor) ○ ○ ○ ○ ○ ○ ○ ○ ○ ○ (great)

Views: (poor) ○ ○ ○ ○ ○ ○ ○ ○ ○ ○ (great)

Enjoyment: (poor) ○ ○ ○ ○ ○ ○ ○ ○ ○ ○ (great)

Notes/pics:

Beinn Eibhinn

Height: 1102m

Date: ....

Ascent start time: .... Peak time: ....

Descent start time: .... Finish time: ....

Ascent duration: .... Descent duration: ....

Total time: [   ]

Total distance covered:...

Companions:..

....

....

Weather conditions:..

....

Difficulty: (poor) ⭕⭕⭕⭕⭕⭕⭕⭕⭕ (great)

Views: (poor) ⭕⭕⭕⭕⭕⭕⭕⭕⭕ (great)

Enjoyment: (poor) ⭕⭕⭕⭕⭕⭕⭕⭕⭕ (great)

Notes/pics:

Beinn Ghlas

Height: 1103m

Date: ....

Ascent start time: .... Peak time: ....

Descent start time: .... Finish time: ....

Ascent duration: .... Descent duration: ....

Total time: [   ]

Total distance covered:..

Companions:...

....

....

Weather conditions:...

....

Difficulty: (poor) ○ ○ ○ ○ ○ ○ ○ ○ ○ ○ (great)

Views: (poor) ○ ○ ○ ○ ○ ○ ○ ○ ○ ○ (great)

Enjoyment: (poor) ○ ○ ○ ○ ○ ○ ○ ○ ○ ○ (great)

Notes/pics:

Stob a'Choire Mheadhoin

Height: 1106m

Date: ....

Ascent start time: .... Peak time: ....

Descent start time: .... Finish time: ....

Ascent duration: .... Descent duration: ....

Total time:

Total distance covered: ....

Companions: ....

....

....

Weather conditions: ....

....

Difficulty: (poor) ○ ○ ○ ○ ○ ○ ○ ○ ○ ○ (great)

Views: (poor) ○ ○ ○ ○ ○ ○ ○ ○ ○ ○ (great)

Enjoyment: (poor) ○ ○ ○ ○ ○ ○ ○ ○ ○ ○ (great)

Notes/pics:

Meall a'Bhuiridh

Height: 1108m

Date: ....
Ascent start time: .... Peak time: ....
Descent start time: .... Finish time: ....

Ascent duration: .... Descent duration: ....

Total time: [   ]

Total distance covered:...

Companions:..

....

....

Weather conditions:..

....

Difficulty: (poor) ○ ○ ○ ○ ○ ○ ○ ○ ○ (great)

Views: (poor) ○ ○ ○ ○ ○ ○ ○ ○ ○ (great)

Enjoyment: (poor) ○ ○ ○ ○ ○ ○ ○ ○ ○ (great)

Notes/pics:

Sgurr nan Conbhairean

Height: 1109m

Date: ....

Ascent start time: .... Peak time: ....

Descent start time: .... Finish time: ....

Ascent duration: .... Descent duration: ....

Total time:

Total distance covered:...

Companions:..

....

....

Weather conditions:..

....

Difficulty: (poor) ○ ○ ○ ○ ○ ○ ○ ○ ○ (great)

Views: (poor) ○ ○ ○ ○ ○ ○ ○ ○ ○ (great)

Enjoyment: (poor) ○ ○ ○ ○ ○ ○ ○ ○ ○ (great)

Notes/pics:

Sgurr Mor

Height: 1110m

Date: ....
Ascent start time: .... Peak time: ....
Descent start time: .... Finish time: ....

Ascent duration: .... Descent duration: ....

Total time: [   ]

Total distance covered:..

Companions:..

....

....

Weather conditions:..

....

Difficulty: (poor) ⭘⭘⭘⭘⭘⭘⭘⭘⭘⭘ (great)

Views: (poor) ⭘⭘⭘⭘⭘⭘⭘⭘⭘⭘ (great)

Enjoyment: (poor) ⭘⭘⭘⭘⭘⭘⭘⭘⭘⭘ (great)

Notes/pics:

Tom a'Choinich

Height: 1112m

Date: ....
Ascent start time: .... Peak time: ....
Descent start time: .... Finish time: ....

Ascent duration: .... Descent duration: ....

Total time:

Total distance covered:..

Companions:..

....

....

Weather conditions:..

....

Difficulty: (poor) ○ ○ ○ ○ ○ ○ ○ ○ ○ (great)

Views: (poor) ○ ○ ○ ○ ○ ○ ○ ○ ○ (great)

Enjoyment: (poor) ○ ○ ○ ○ ○ ○ ○ ○ ○ (great)

Notes/pics:

Monadh Mor

Height: 1113m

Date: ....

Ascent start time: .... Peak time: ....

Descent start time: .... Finish time: ....

Ascent duration: .... Descent duration: ....

Total time: [   ]

Total distance covered: ....

Companions: ....

....

....

Weather conditions: ....

....

Difficulty: (poor) ○ ○ ○ ○ ○ ○ ○ ○ ○ ○ (great)

Views: (poor) ○ ○ ○ ○ ○ ○ ○ ○ ○ ○ (great)

Enjoyment: (poor) ○ ○ ○ ○ ○ ○ ○ ○ ○ ○ (great)

Notes/pics:

Stob Coire Easain

Height: 1115m

Date: ....

Ascent start time: .... Peak time: ....

Descent start time: .... Finish time: ....

Ascent duration: .... Descent duration: ....

Total time:

Total distance covered:..

Companions:..

....

....

Weather conditions:..

....

Difficulty: (poor) O O O O O O O O O O (great)

Views: (poor) O O O O O O O O O O (great)

Enjoyment: (poor) O O O O O O O O O O (great)

Notes/pics:

Stob Coire an Laoigh

Height: 1116m

Date: ....

Ascent start time: .... Peak time: ....

Descent start time: .... Finish time: ....

Ascent duration: .... Descent duration: ....

Total time:

Total distance covered:...

Companions:...

....

....

Weather conditions:..

....

Difficulty: (poor) ○ ○ ○ ○ ○ ○ ○ ○ ○ (great)

Views: (poor) ○ ○ ○ ○ ○ ○ ○ ○ ○ (great)

Enjoyment: (poor) ○ ○ ○ ○ ○ ○ ○ ○ ○ (great)

Notes/pics:

Aonach Beag (Alder)

Height: 1116m

Date: ....

Ascent start time: .... Peak time: ....

Descent start time: .... Finish time: ....

Ascent duration: .... Descent duration: ....

Total time:

Total distance covered:..

Companions:...

....

....

Weather conditions:...

....

Difficulty: (poor) ○ ○ ○ ○ ○ ○ ○ ○ ○ (great)

Views: (poor) ○ ○ ○ ○ ○ ○ ○ ○ ○ (great)

Enjoyment: (poor) ○ ○ ○ ○ ○ ○ ○ ○ ○ (great)

Notes/pics:

Sgor Gaoith

Height: 1118m

Date: ....

Ascent start time: .... Peak time: ....

Descent start time: .... Finish time: ....

Ascent duration: .... Descent duration: ....

Total time: [   ]

Total distance covered: ....

Companions: ....

....

....

Weather conditions: ....

....

Difficulty: (poor) ○ ○ ○ ○ ○ ○ ○ ○ ○ ○ (great)

Views: (poor) ○ ○ ○ ○ ○ ○ ○ ○ ○ ○ (great)

Enjoyment: (poor) ○ ○ ○ ○ ○ ○ ○ ○ ○ ○ (great)

Notes/pics:

Meall Garbh
(Ben Lawers)

Height: 1118m

Date: ....

Ascent start time: .... Peak time: ....

Descent start time: .... Finish time: ....

Ascent duration: .... Descent duration: ....

Total time: [   ]

Total distance covered:...

Companions:..

....

....

Weather conditions:...

....

Difficulty: (poor) ○ ○ ○ ○ ○ ○ ○ ○ ○ ○ (great)

Views: (poor) ○ ○ ○ ○ ○ ○ ○ ○ ○ ○ (great)

Enjoyment: (poor) ○ ○ ○ ○ ○ ○ ○ ○ ○ ○ (great)

Notes/pics:

Carn a'Choire Bhoidheach

Height: 1118m

Date: ....

Ascent start time: .... Peak time: ....

Descent start time: .... Finish time: ....

Ascent duration: .... Descent duration: ....

Total time: ☐

Total distance covered: ....

Companions: ....

....

....

Weather conditions: ....

....

Difficulty: (poor) ○ ○ ○ ○ ○ ○ ○ ○ ○ ○ (great)

Views: (poor) ○ ○ ○ ○ ○ ○ ○ ○ ○ ○ (great)

Enjoyment: (poor) ○ ○ ○ ○ ○ ○ ○ ○ ○ ○ (great)

Notes/pics:

An Stuc

Height: 1118m

Date: ....

Ascent start time: .... Peak time: ....

Descent start time: .... Finish time: ....

Ascent duration: .... Descent duration: ....

Total time:

Total distance covered:..

Companions:...

....

....

Weather conditions:..

....

Difficulty: (poor) ○ ○ ○ ○ ○ ○ ○ ○ ○ ○ (great)

Views: (poor) ○ ○ ○ ○ ○ ○ ○ ○ ○ ○ (great)

Enjoyment: (poor) ○ ○ ○ ○ ○ ○ ○ ○ ○ ○ (great)

Notes/pics:

A' Chralaig

Height: 1120m

Date: ....

Ascent start time: .... Peak time: ....

Descent start time: .... Finish time: ....

Ascent duration: .... Descent duration: ....

Total time: [   ]

Total distance covered:...

Companions:..

....

....

Weather conditions:...

....

Difficulty: (poor) ○ ○ ○ ○ ○ ○ ○ ○ ○ ○ (great)

Views: (poor) ○ ○ ○ ○ ○ ○ ○ ○ ○ ○ (great)

Enjoyment: (poor) ○ ○ ○ ○ ○ ○ ○ ○ ○ ○ (great)

Notes/pics:

Carn nan Gabhar

Height: 1121m

Date: ....

Ascent start time: .... Peak time: ....

Descent start time: .... Finish time: ....

Ascent duration: .... Descent duration: ....

Total time: [   ]

Total distance covered: ....

Companions: ....

....

....

Weather conditions: ....

....

Difficulty: (poor) ○ ○ ○ ○ ○ ○ ○ ○ ○ ○ (great)

Views: (poor) ○ ○ ○ ○ ○ ○ ○ ○ ○ ○ (great)

Enjoyment: (poor) ○ ○ ○ ○ ○ ○ ○ ○ ○ ○ (great)

Notes/pics:

Ben Cruachan

Height: 1126m

Date: ....

Ascent start time: .... Peak time: ....

Descent start time: .... Finish time: ....

Ascent duration: .... Descent duration: ....

Total time: ☐

Total distance covered:..

Companions:...

....

....

Weather conditions:...

....

Difficulty: (poor) ○ ○ ○ ○ ○ ○ ○ ○ ○ ○ (great)

Views: (poor) ○ ○ ○ ○ ○ ○ ○ ○ ○ ○ (great)

Enjoyment: (poor) ○ ○ ○ ○ ○ ○ ○ ○ ○ ○ (great)

Notes/pics:

An Riabhachan

Height: 1129m

Date: ....

Ascent start time: .... Peak time: ....

Descent start time: .... Finish time: ....

Ascent duration: .... Descent duration: ....

Total time: [   ]

Total distance covered:..

Companions:..

....

....

Weather conditions:..

....

Difficulty:　(poor) ○ ○ ○ ○ ○ ○ ○ ○ ○ (great)

Views:　　　(poor) ○ ○ ○ ○ ○ ○ ○ ○ ○ (great)

Enjoyment: (poor) ○ ○ ○ ○ ○ ○ ○ ○ ○ (great)

Notes/pics:

Creag Meagaidh

Height: 1130m

Date: ....

Ascent start time: .... Peak time: ....

Descent start time: .... Finish time: ....

Ascent duration: .... Descent duration: ....

Total time: [   ]

Total distance covered:...

Companions:..

....

....

Weather conditions:..

....

Difficulty: (poor) ○ ○ ○ ○ ○ ○ ○ ○ ○ ○ (great)

Views: (poor) ○ ○ ○ ○ ○ ○ ○ ○ ○ ○ (great)

Enjoyment: (poor) ○ ○ ○ ○ ○ ○ ○ ○ ○ ○ (great)

Notes/pics:

Binnein Mor

Height: 1130m

Date: ....

Ascent start time: .... Peak time: ....

Descent start time: .... Finish time: ....

Ascent duration: .... Descent duration: ....

Total time:

Total distance covered: ....

Companions: ....

....

....

Weather conditions: ....

....

Difficulty: (poor) ○ ○ ○ ○ ○ ○ ○ ○ ○ ○ (great)

Views: (poor) ○ ○ ○ ○ ○ ○ ○ ○ ○ ○ (great)

Enjoyment: (poor) ○ ○ ○ ○ ○ ○ ○ ○ ○ ○ (great)

Notes/pics:

Ben Lui

Height: 1130m

Date: ....

Ascent start time: .... Peak time: ....

Descent start time: .... Finish time: ....

Ascent duration: .... Descent duration: ....

Total time:

Total distance covered:...

Companions:...

....

....

Weather conditions:...

....

Difficulty: (poor) ○ ○ ○ ○ ○ ○ ○ ○ ○ ○ (great)

Views: (poor) ○ ○ ○ ○ ○ ○ ○ ○ ○ ○ (great)

Enjoyment: (poor) ○ ○ ○ ○ ○ ○ ○ ○ ○ ○ (great)

Notes/pics:

Geal-charn
(Alder)

Height: 1132m

Date: ....

Ascent start time: .... Peak time: ....

Descent start time: .... Finish time: ....

Ascent duration: .... Descent duration: ....

Total time:

Total distance covered:...

Companions:...

....

....

Weather conditions:...

....

Difficulty: (poor) ○ ○ ○ ○ ○ ○ ○ ○ ○ ○ (great)

Views: (poor) ○ ○ ○ ○ ○ ○ ○ ○ ○ ○ (great)

Enjoyment: (poor) ○ ○ ○ ○ ○ ○ ○ ○ ○ ○ (great)

Notes/pics:

Ben Alder

Height: 1148m

Date: ....
Ascent start time: .... Peak time: ....
Descent start time: .... Finish time: ....

Ascent duration: .... Descent duration: ....

Total time: ⌈_____⌉

Total distance covered:..

Companions:...

....

....

Weather conditions:..

....

Difficulty: (poor) ○ ○ ○ ○ ○ ○ ○ ○ ○ ○ (great)

Views: (poor) ○ ○ ○ ○ ○ ○ ○ ○ ○ ○ (great)

Enjoyment: (poor) ○ ○ ○ ○ ○ ○ ○ ○ ○ ○ (great)

Notes/pics:

Sgurr na Lapaich

Height: 1150m

Date: ....

Ascent start time: .... Peak time: ....

Descent start time: .... Finish time: ....

Ascent duration: .... Descent duration: ....

Total time: [ ]

Total distance covered:...

Companions:...

....

....

Weather conditions:..

....

Difficulty: (poor) ○ ○ ○ ○ ○ ○ ○ ○ ○ ○ (great)

Views: (poor) ○ ○ ○ ○ ○ ○ ○ ○ ○ ○ (great)

Enjoyment: (poor) ○ ○ ○ ○ ○ ○ ○ ○ ○ ○ (great)

Notes/pics:

Bidean nam Bian

Height: 1150m

Date: ....

Ascent start time: .... Peak time: ....

Descent start time: .... Finish time: ....

Ascent duration: .... Descent duration: ....

Total time:

Total distance covered: ....

Companions: ....

....

....

Weather conditions: ....

....

Difficulty: (poor) ○○○○○○○○○○ (great)

Views: (poor) ○○○○○○○○○○ (great)

Enjoyment: (poor) ○○○○○○○○○○ (great)

Notes/pics:

Sgurr nan Ceathreamhnan

Height: 1151m

Date: ....

Ascent start time: .... Peak time: ....

Descent start time: .... Finish time: ....

Ascent duration: .... Descent duration: ....

Total time:

Total distance covered:...

Companions:...

....

....

Weather conditions:...

....

Difficulty: (poor) O O O O O O O O O O (great)

Views: (poor) O O O O O O O O O O (great)

Enjoyment: (poor) O O O O O O O O O O (great)

Notes/pics:

Lochnagar

Height: 1155m

Date: ....

Ascent start time: .... Peak time: ....

Descent start time: .... Finish time: ....

Ascent duration: .... Descent duration: ....

Total time: ☐

Total distance covered:..

Companions:...

....

....

Weather conditions:...

....

Difficulty: (poor) ○ ○ ○ ○ ○ ○ ○ ○ ○ ○ (great)

Views: (poor) ○ ○ ○ ○ ○ ○ ○ ○ ○ ○ (great)

Enjoyment: (poor) ○ ○ ○ ○ ○ ○ ○ ○ ○ ○ (great)

Notes/pics:

Derry Cairngorm

Height: 1155m

Date: ....

Ascent start time: .... Peak time: ....

Descent start time: .... Finish time: ....

Ascent duration: .... Descent duration: ....

Total time: [ ]

Total distance covered:...

Companions:...

....

....

Weather conditions:...

....

Difficulty: (poor) ○ ○ ○ ○ ○ ○ ○ ○ ○ ○ (great)

Views: (poor) ○ ○ ○ ○ ○ ○ ○ ○ ○ ○ (great)

Enjoyment: (poor) ○ ○ ○ ○ ○ ○ ○ ○ ○ ○ (great)

Notes/pics:

Beinn Bhrotain

Height: 1157m

Date: ....

Ascent start time: .... Peak time: ....

Descent start time: .... Finish time: ....

Ascent duration: .... Descent duration: ....

Total time:

Total distance covered:...

Companions:...

....

....

Weather conditions:...

....

Difficulty:　(poor) ○ ○ ○ ○ ○ ○ ○ ○ ○ (great)

Views:　(poor) ○ ○ ○ ○ ○ ○ ○ ○ ○ (great)

Enjoyment: (poor) ○ ○ ○ ○ ○ ○ ○ ○ ○ (great)

Notes/pics:

Stob Binnein

Height: 1165m

Date: ....

Ascent start time: .... Peak time: ....

Descent start time: .... Finish time: ....

Ascent duration: .... Descent duration: ....

Total time: [   ]

Total distance covered:...

Companions:...

....

....

Weather conditions:..

....

Difficulty: (poor) O O O O O O O O O (great)

Views: (poor) O O O O O O O O O (great)

Enjoyment: (poor) O O O O O O O O O (great)

Notes/pics:

Ben Avon

Height: 1171m

Date: ....

Ascent start time: .... Peak time: ....

Descent start time: .... Finish time: ....

Ascent duration: .... Descent duration: ....

Total time: [   ]

Total distance covered:...

Companions:...

....

....

Weather conditions:...

....

Difficulty: (poor) ○ ○ ○ ○ ○ ○ ○ ○ ○ ○ (great)

Views: (poor) ○ ○ ○ ○ ○ ○ ○ ○ ○ ○ (great)

Enjoyment: (poor) ○ ○ ○ ○ ○ ○ ○ ○ ○ ○ (great)

Notes/pics:

Ben More

Height: 1174m

Date: ....

Ascent start time: .... Peak time: ....

Descent start time: .... Finish time: ....

Ascent duration: .... Descent duration: ....

Total time:

Total distance covered:..

Companions:...

....

....

Weather conditions:...

....

Difficulty: (poor) ○ ○ ○ ○ ○ ○ ○ ○ ○ ○ (great)

Views: (poor) ○ ○ ○ ○ ○ ○ ○ ○ ○ ○ (great)

Enjoyment: (poor) ○ ○ ○ ○ ○ ○ ○ ○ ○ ○ (great)

Notes/pics:

Stob Choire Claurigh

Height: 1177m

Date: ....

Ascent start time: .... Peak time: ....

Descent start time: .... Finish time: ....

Ascent duration: .... Descent duration: ....

Total time:

Total distance covered:..

Companions:...

....

....

Weather conditions:..

....

Difficulty: (poor) ○ ○ ○ ○ ○ ○ ○ ○ ○ ○ (great)

Views: (poor) ○ ○ ○ ○ ○ ○ ○ ○ ○ ○ (great)

Enjoyment: (poor) ○ ○ ○ ○ ○ ○ ○ ○ ○ ○ (great)

Notes/pics:

Mam Sodhail

Height: 1181m

Date: ....

Ascent start time: .... Peak time: ....

Descent start time: .... Finish time: ....

Ascent duration: .... Descent duration: ....

Total time: [   ]

Total distance covered:..

Companions:..

....

....

Weather conditions:..

....

Difficulty: (poor) ○ ○ ○ ○ ○ ○ ○ ○ ○ ○ (great)

Views: (poor) ○ ○ ○ ○ ○ ○ ○ ○ ○ ○ (great)

Enjoyment: (poor) ○ ○ ○ ○ ○ ○ ○ ○ ○ ○ (great)

Notes/pics:

Beinn Mheadhoin

Height: 1182m

Date: ....

Ascent start time: .... Peak time: ....

Descent start time: .... Finish time: ....

Ascent duration: .... Descent duration: ....

Total time: [ ]

Total distance covered: ....

Companions: ....

....

....

Weather conditions: ....

....

Difficulty: (poor) ○ ○ ○ ○ ○ ○ ○ ○ ○ (great)

Views: (poor) ○ ○ ○ ○ ○ ○ ○ ○ ○ (great)

Enjoyment: (poor) ○ ○ ○ ○ ○ ○ ○ ○ ○ (great)

Notes/pics:

Carn Eige

Height: 1183m

Date: ....

Ascent start time: .... Peak time: ....

Descent start time: .... Finish time: ....

Ascent duration: .... Descent duration: ....

Total time: [   ]

Total distance covered:..

Companions:...

....

....

Weather conditions:...

....

Difficulty: (poor) ○ ○ ○ ○ ○ ○ ○ ○ ○ (great)

Views: (poor) ○ ○ ○ ○ ○ ○ ○ ○ ○ (great)

Enjoyment: (poor) ○ ○ ○ ○ ○ ○ ○ ○ ○ (great)

Notes/pics:

Beinn a'Bhuird

Height: 1197m

Date: ....
Ascent start time: .... Peak time: ....
Descent start time: .... Finish time: ....

Ascent duration: .... Descent duration: ....
Total time: [   ]
Total distance covered:..
Companions:..
....
....
Weather conditions:...
....

Difficulty: (poor) ○ ○ ○ ○ ○ ○ ○ ○ ○ ○ (great)
Views: (poor) ○ ○ ○ ○ ○ ○ ○ ○ ○ ○ (great)
Enjoyment: (poor) ○ ○ ○ ○ ○ ○ ○ ○ ○ ○ (great)

Notes/pics:

Ben Lawers

Height: 1214m

Date: ....

Ascent start time: .... Peak time: ....

Descent start time: .... Finish time: ....

Ascent duration: .... Descent duration: ....

Total time: [   ]

Total distance covered:..

Companions:...

....

....

Weather conditions:...

....

Difficulty: (poor) ○ ○ ○ ○ ○ ○ ○ ○ ○ ○ (great)

Views: (poor) ○ ○ ○ ○ ○ ○ ○ ○ ○ ○ (great)

Enjoyment: (poor) ○ ○ ○ ○ ○ ○ ○ ○ ○ ○ (great)

Notes/pics:

Carn Mor Dearg

Height: 1220m

Date: ....

Ascent start time: .... Peak time: ....

Descent start time: .... Finish time: ....

Ascent duration: .... Descent duration: ....

Total time:

Total distance covered:..

Companions:..

....

....

Weather conditions:...

....

Difficulty:　(poor) ○ ○ ○ ○ ○ ○ ○ ○ ○ ○ (great)

Views:　　　(poor) ○ ○ ○ ○ ○ ○ ○ ○ ○ ○ (great)

Enjoyment: (poor) ○ ○ ○ ○ ○ ○ ○ ○ ○ ○ (great)

Notes/pics:

Aonach Mor

Height: 1221m

Date: ....

Ascent start time: .... Peak time: ....

Descent start time: .... Finish time: ....

Ascent duration: .... Descent duration: ....

Total time: [   ]

Total distance covered:...

Companions:...

....

....

Weather conditions:..

....

Difficulty: (poor) O O O O O O O O O O (great)

Views: (poor) O O O O O O O O O O (great)

Enjoyment: (poor) O O O O O O O O O O (great)

· Notes/pics:

Aonach Beag
(Nevis Range)

Height: 1234m

Date: ....

Ascent start time: .... Peak time: ....

Descent start time: .... Finish time: ....

Ascent duration: .... Descent duration: ....

Total time:

Total distance covered: ....

Companions: ....

....

....

Weather conditions: ....

....

Difficulty: (poor) ○ ○ ○ ○ ○ ○ ○ ○ ○ ○ (great)

Views: (poor) ○ ○ ○ ○ ○ ○ ○ ○ ○ ○ (great)

Enjoyment: (poor) ○ ○ ○ ○ ○ ○ ○ ○ ○ ○ (great)

Notes/pics:

Cairn Gorm

Height: 1245m

Date: ....

Ascent start time: .... Peak time: ....

Descent start time: .... Finish time: ....

Ascent duration: .... Descent duration: ....

Total time:

Total distance covered: ....

Companions: ....

....

....

Weather conditions: ....

....

Difficulty: (poor) ⭘ ⭘ ⭘ ⭘ ⭘ ⭘ ⭘ ⭘ ⭘ (great)

Views: (poor) ⭘ ⭘ ⭘ ⭘ ⭘ ⭘ ⭘ ⭘ ⭘ (great)

Enjoyment: (poor) ⭘ ⭘ ⭘ ⭘ ⭘ ⭘ ⭘ ⭘ ⭘ (great)

Notes/pics:

Sgor an Lochain Uaine

Height: 1258m

Date: ....

Ascent start time: .... Peak time: ....

Descent start time: .... Finish time: ....

Ascent duration: .... Descent duration: ....

Total time: [ ]

Total distance covered: ....

Companions: ....

....

....

Weather conditions: ....

....

Difficulty: (poor) ○ ○ ○ ○ ○ ○ ○ ○ ○ ○ (great)

Views: (poor) ○ ○ ○ ○ ○ ○ ○ ○ ○ ○ (great)

Enjoyment: (poor) ○ ○ ○ ○ ○ ○ ○ ○ ○ ○ (great)

Notes/pics:

Cairn Toul

Height: 1291m

Date: ....

Ascent start time: .... Peak time: ....

Descent start time: .... Finish time: ....

Ascent duration: .... Descent duration: ....

Total time: [   ]

Total distance covered:...

Companions:...

....

....

Weather conditions:..

....

Difficulty: (poor) ○ ○ ○ ○ ○ ○ ○ ○ ○ ○ (great)

Views: (poor) ○ ○ ○ ○ ○ ○ ○ ○ ○ ○ (great)

Enjoyment: (poor) ○ ○ ○ ○ ○ ○ ○ ○ ○ ○ (great)

Notes/pics:

Braeriach

Height: 1296m

Date: ....

Ascent start time: .... Peak time: ....

Descent start time: .... Finish time: ....

Ascent duration: .... Descent duration: ....

Total time: [   ]

Total distance covered:...

Companions:...

....

....

Weather conditions:...

....

Difficulty: (poor) O O O O O O O O O O (great)

Views: (poor) O O O O O O O O O O (great)

Enjoyment: (poor) O O O O O O O O O O (great)

Notes/pics:

Ben Macdui

Height: 1309m

Date: ....

Ascent start time: .... Peak time: ....

Descent start time: .... Finish time: ....

Ascent duration: .... Descent duration: ....

Total time: [   ]

Total distance covered: ....

Companions: ....

....

....

Weather conditions: ....

....

Difficulty: (poor) ○ ○ ○ ○ ○ ○ ○ ○ ○ ○ (great)

Views: (poor) ○ ○ ○ ○ ○ ○ ○ ○ ○ ○ (great)

Enjoyment: (poor) ○ ○ ○ ○ ○ ○ ○ ○ ○ ○ (great)

Notes/pics:

Ben Nevis

Height: 1345m

Date: ....

Ascent start time: .... Peak time: ....

Descent start time: .... Finish time: ....

Ascent duration: .... Descent duration: ....

Total time: [ ]

Total distance covered:...

Companions:...

....

....

Weather conditions:...

....

Difficulty: (poor) ○ ○ ○ ○ ○ ○ ○ ○ ○ ○ (great)

Views: (poor) ○ ○ ○ ○ ○ ○ ○ ○ ○ ○ (great)

Enjoyment: (poor) ○ ○ ○ ○ ○ ○ ○ ○ ○ ○ (great)

Notes/pics:

Notes & Emergency Contact Numbers

Hikers Name

Emergency Contact Name

Emergency Contact No

Munro Finder (A to Z)

Printed in Great Britain
by Amazon

62708438R00163